Growing Citrus

Growing Citrus

The Essential Gardener's Guide

Martin Page

Timber Press
Portland | London

◀ Frontispiece: 'Owari' Satsuma.

Published in 2008 by
Timber Press, Inc.

The Haseltine Building
133 S.W. Second Avenue, Suite 450
Portland, Oregon 97204-3527
www.timberpress.com

2 The Quadrant
135 Salusbury Road
London NW6 6RJ
www.timberpress.co.uk

Design by Dick Malt
Printed in China

Library of Congress Cataloging-in-Publication Data
Page, Martin, 1953-
  Growing citrus : the essential gardener's guide / Martin Page.
       p. cm.
  Includes bibliographical references and index.
  ISBN-13: 978-0-88192-906-5
  1. Citrus. 2. Citrus fruits. I. Title.
  SB369.P24 2009
  634'.304--dc22
                                        2008016960

A catalogue record for this book is also available from the
British Library.

Contents

Acknowledgements 7

1 **Introduction** 9

2 **Origin and History** 13

3 **Botany and Taxonomy** 25

4 **Economic Uses of Citrus Fruit** 35

5 **Soil and Nutrition** 49

6 **Growing Citrus Trees** 59

7 **Pests and Diseases** 81

8 **An Encyclopedia of Citrus** 97

    Sweet Orange 98   **Kumquats** 139

    Mandarins 107   **Limequats** 142

    Citrangequats 119   **Sour Orange** 144

    Grapefruit 119   **Bergamot** 146

    Pummelo 124   **Tangelo** 147

    Lemons 129   **New Zealand Grapefruit** 147

    Limes 134   **Australian Dessert Lime** 148

    Citrons 138   **Eremolemons** 149

9 **Citrus Rootstocks** 151

Appendix A Questions and Answers 157
Appendix B Where to See Citrus 160
Appendix C Suppliers 168
Glossary 176
Bibliography 179
Index 184

For my mother

'Oranges and lemons', say the bells of St. Clement's.
'You owe me five farthings', say the bells of St. Martin's.
'When will you pay me?' say the bells of Old Bailey.
'When I grow rich', say the bells of Shoreditch.

'When will that be?' say the bells of Stepney.
'I do not know', says the great bell of Bow.
Here comes a candle to light you to bed
And here comes a chopper to cut off your head!

from a 17th-century English nursery rhyme

Acknowledgements

I would like to thank the following people for their help during the preparation of this book: Tracy Kahn, Curator of the Citrus Collection at the University of California, Riverside; Richard F. Lee and Robert R. Krueger of the United States Department of Agriculture National Clonal Germplasm Repository for Citrus and Dates, Riverside, California; Kasha and David Furman of Cricket Hill Garden, Thomaston, Connecticut; Claire Austin and Ric Kenwood of Claire Austin Hardy Plants, Edgebolton, Shropshire; Tim Rassell and his family at Rassell's Nursery, Little Bytham, Lincolnshire; Patricia Oliver of Global Orange Groves, Poole, Dorset; Luciana Carotenuto of Italy; Jorma Koskinen of Finland; and Panna Richey.

I would also like to thank the staff of the Bodleian Library and the Department of Plant Sciences, Oxford University, for permitting access to their collections; Barbara Collecott from the Royal Horticultural Society's Lindley Library; Plymouth City Council for permission to use photographs of Mount Edgcumbe; the University of California, Riverside, for permission to photograph citrus trees in their collection; and the Royal Botanic Gardens, Kew.

Citrus trees at the Alfabia gardens of Majorca. These gardens trace their origin to Arabs who selected the site between the fourteenth and fifteenth centuries.

1 Introduction

Citrus trees must have seemed incredibly exotic to the people of medieval Europe. Citrons had been known for some time, but the advent of the sweet orange must have come as a shock and opened up a completely new vista of culinary opportunity.

The Arab peoples of the Middle East are generally credited with bringing the plants from Asia. In the early Middle Ages the majority of Spain and Portugal was under Arab control. Gradually the fruit made its way further west, following military conquests or simply through trading. Oranges and lemons must have commanded high prices in the bazaars of the Middle East, and the Arabs must have recognised the value of this golden crop.

The lemon, lime, sour, and ultimately the sweet orange eventually made their way onto the tables of western Europe. In doing so they stimulated an interest for growing tender plants in a cold climate and had a major impact on the architecture of the garden. While citrus trees could be grown outside in southern Italy, this was not the case further north, and walled gardens were created to protect the tender plants.

The Arabs were sophisticated people, the guardians of the knowledge of the Greeks, Egyptians, Romans, and other ancient Mediterranean civilisations. They built the incredibly beautiful Alhambra Palace in Seville and, presumably, grew orchards of citrus trees. The new fruit also had an impact upon western European culture. Oranges were so highly valued that wealthy landowners were willing to spend substantial amounts of money erecting special buildings to protect them. This led to the creation of a completely new type of structure, the orangery. The impact of these buildings is still felt today.

The Middle Ages was a period when there were no tomatoes, bananas, sweet peppers, or sweet corn. Potatoes had yet to be discovered, so there were no French fries. Spices were available from India, but they were extremely expensive and most people relied upon herbs such as rosemary, thyme, and mint to flavour their food. To this bland culinary world came an exciting new fruit. There was nothing else like it. It was sweet, beautifully flavoured, and bright orange in colour. No wonder the wealthy land owners wanted to grow it for themselves and impress their friends and political competitors.

From a personal perspective, I have been growing citrus trees for over twenty years and they have given me considerable pleasure. All of my trees are containerised, but I have also grown them in the borders of a greenhouse and have been amazed at how tolerant they are. Citrus trees will not survive being frozen, but most will withstand much lower temperatures than is generally believed. Plant breeders have also developed several citrus hybrids that will cope with much lower temperatures than conventional commercial varieties such as oranges and lemons.

Many of these hybrids have rather intimidating names, but there is a simple formula to working out their parentage. For example, crossing a lime with a kumquat produced a limequat (lime + quat) and crossing a tangerine with an orange created a tangor (tang + or). The term *tangerine* is often used to describe what is technically a mandarin, but it was originally coined to describe the 'Dancy' mandarin, because most of the fruit at that time originated from Tangiers. All clementines and tangerines are types of mandarin citrus—known botanically as *Citrus reticulata* (according to Swingle's classification). Some well-known cultivars are actually hybrids between two species. 'Meyer' lemon, for example, is a hybrid between a lemon and either a mandarin or a sweet orange. An explanation of the most common terms can be found in the glossary at the back of this book.

Over the years I have found that citrus are remarkably tolerant, but a visitor from California would be amazed at the lengths to which I have to go to keep my plants alive. However, once you understand their basic requirements, there is no great secret to growing these fascinating plants—but it does help if you are relatively fit. The main pre-requisite to growing citrus trees in a temperate climate is a bright and frost-free place in which to grow them during the winter. The range of plants that can be grown depends more upon the minimum temperature that can be maintained in the winter than how hot it is in the summer. Citrus trees will thrive in the border of an unheated greenhouse during the summer, but it can cost a significant amount of money to keep the greenhouse heated during the winter.

Global warming is likely to have a major effect upon how we garden in the future. Some countries will benefit from the warmer conditions, while

◀ 'Ellendale' mandarin is thought to be a tangor, a hybrid between a sweet orange and a mandarin.

▲ 'Murcott' tangor, also known as honey tangerine, is very cold hardy and produces plenty of fruit.

▶ 'Murcott' fruit is very sweet-tasting.

others will suffer with an increasing incidence of drought. This change in climate has major implications for gardeners, but those in colder countries will be able to grow plants that were previously considered to be too tender.

One of the main advantages of growing your own citrus fruit is that you know what they have been sprayed with. Commercially grown citrus fruit go through a complex process prior to sale. The fruit are rinsed with water and cleaned with rotating horsehair brushes, which remove most of the dirt, mould-causing fungi, and insects from the surface. The remainder of the dirt and any persistent chemicals are then removed by spraying the fruit with a detergent. Unfortunately, this also removes the naturally occurring waxes, which have to be replaced by spraying the fruit with an edible wax, such as Carnauba or the naturally occurring polymer shellac. The fruit are finally sprayed with a fungicide to prevent post-harvest decay. The fungicides are applied in aqueous form or dissolved in the wax. Artificial colour is sometimes added to the fruit when they are harvested early in the season. This only affects the surface of the fruit.

Organic fruit, or fruit collected from your own trees, often have considerably more fragrance than fruit sold in a supermarket. The scent is elusive, but extremely pleasant. Your neighbours might think that you are rather strange, but sniffing fruit is one of the pleasures of growing citrus plants.

2 Origin and History

Today we can only imagine the impact that sweet oranges had when they reached western Europe at the beginning of the sixteenth century. The pinnacle of interest in citrus occurred after the end of the Eighty Years War (1568–1648), when the Netherlands achieved independence from Spain. The war had involved many other countries and made European travel very dangerous. Wealthy people were attracted to the exotic fruit and constructed purpose-built orangeries to house their new plants.

Little is known about the origins of the first cultivars of citrus, but the Chinese had been growing oranges for hundreds of years before they came to the attention of Europeans. The first written work about citrus fruit seems to be *Ju Lu* by Han Yanzhi in 1178 A.D. In this book he describes 28 kinds of citrus and how to cultivate them (Needham 1986). The Cultural Revolution almost destroyed the citrus industry in China and Chairman Mao (Mao Zedong) demanded the destruction of all orange trees. Mao's successor, Deng Xiaoping, by contrast, recognised the value of the industry and ordered the replanting of the orchards (Valder 1999).

Citron

Citrus plants first appear in Western literature in approximately 310 B.C. when the Greek philosopher Theophrastus described the citron in *Historia Plantarum*. Theophrastus believed that the plant originated from the land of the Medes, the area roughly corresponding today with northwestern Iran, Kurdistan, and Azarbaijan. 'Thus one sees in Media and Persia among many other productions the tree called the Persian or Median-apple'. The citron is mentioned several times in early Greek and Jewish literature and appears to have been widely cultivated.

The citron may have found its way to Europe by peaceful means, but most authors believe that the Greeks collected it when Alexander the Great

invaded India in 326 B.C. The Macedonians reached as far as the Indus River and they must have found many unusual plants in India. The citron was certainly the first citrus fruit to reach the continent of Europe. It appears on coins, paintings, and statues and is illustrated in a mosaic at the Church of the Nativity in Bethlehem.

Pliny the Elder (Gaius Plinius Secundus) was probably familiar with the citron when he wrote his *Natural History* in the first century A.D., although he is known to have borrowed extensively from other people's work. In Book XIII, titled *Natural History of Exotic Trees*, he wrote:

There is another tree also which has the same name of 'citrus', and bears a fruit that is held by some persons in particular dislike for its smell and remarkable bitterness; while, on the other hand, there are some who esteem it very highly. This tree is used as an ornament to houses; it requires, however, no further description.

Elsewhere Pliny (Book XII, *Natural History of Trees*) wrote that the fruit

is never eaten, but it is remarkable for its extremely powerful smell, which is the case, also, with the leaves; indeed, the odour is so strong, that it will penetrate clothes, when they are once impregnated with it, and hence it is very useful in repelling the attacks of noxious insects. The tree bears fruit at all seasons of the year; while some is falling off, other fruit is ripening, and other, again, just bursting into birth. Various nations have attempted to naturalise this tree among them, for the sake of its medical properties, by planting it in pots of clay, with holes drilled in them, for the purpose of introducing the air to the roots.

The last part of Pliny's statement is very interesting because it is obvious that the citrus tree has a long history as a potted plant.

Lemon

The origin of the lemon has always been uncertain, but strong evidence indicates that the Romans were growing it as early as the first century. Until recently, most authors believed that the ancient Romans were unaware of the lemon, suggesting instead that it first reached Europe during the Middle Ages. However, in 1951 excavations in the ancient Roman city of Pompeii revealed a wall painting of what appears to be a lemon tree. The fresco in the House of the Orchard clearly shows bright yellow, spindle-shaped fruit, held upright on a tree, rather than hanging down, as citrons would have done. We know that Vesuvius destroyed the city in 79 A.D., which would definitely suggest that the Romans, or at least the fresco painter, had seen lemons at some time prior to that date.

China is the most likely origin of the lemon, although this is impossible to prove with any certainty. There are several references to it coming from the 'southern barbarians', but it is unclear whether this refers to southern China or to countries beyond its borders. The Arabs had certainly introduced the lemon and the sour orange to Palestine and Persia by the beginning of the twelfth century and from there the fruit found their way to other Arab possessions in Spain and North Africa.

The distribution of many plants has depended upon wars and the colonisation of other countries, and citrus trees are no exception. In 1095 Pope Urban II launched the First Crusade, with the intention of retrieving Jerusalem and the Holy Land from the Muslims. Thousands of Christian soldiers were sent to Palestine, where they probably found citrus fruit growing in the countryside. Fruit pips take up very little space, so it seems likely that the crusaders would have taken them home and planted them.

The Christians finally conquered Granada in 1492 and reunited the whole of Spain. It seems likely that a range of citrus trees was already growing there and that the new colonists would have continued to cultivate them as the Moors had done previously. Eventually Spain and Portugal would colonise most of the New World and introduce citrus fruit to the Americas.

Sour Orange

The origins of the sour orange are better documented than most of the other species of citrus. According to Gallesio (1811), the plant was collected in India and taken to Oman at some time after 922 A.D. The Arabs then took it to Iraq, Syria, Palestine, and Egypt. The sour orange reached Sicily in 1002, and it was reported as growing around Seville, in Spain, at the end of the twelfth century (Webber and Batchelor 1943).

For many years the sour orange was the only citrus tree grown in Europe. The first orangeries were built for it, and it was only later that they were used to grow the sweet orange. Risso and Poiteau (1818–1822) described 22 cultivars of sour orange, but several of them were very similar and probably wouldn't be recognised as such today. At least two of the cultivars ('Bizzaria' and 'Fasciata') are chimeras and combine the genetic material of two different plants. The original fascination for the sour orange evaporated when the sweet orange was introduced, and most landowners started to grow the sweet orange instead. However, the sour orange still found a role as a landscape tree in the Mediterranean, and it continues to be cultivated today for marmalade and its essential oils.

Mandarin

Mandarins have been cultivated in China for many centuries but were not introduced into Europe until 1805, when Sir Abraham Hume (1748–1838) managed to acquire a couple of specimens from Canton (now Guangzhou). The British East India Company had a long-established trading post in Canton, where it traded silver for tea. No one knows how the English managed to obtain the mandarin plants, but presumably the plants were traded for silver or some other commodity. Hume, one of the leading plant collectors of his day, seems to have had an uncanny ability to obtain rare Chinese plants. He was a Fellow of the Royal Society and a founding member of the Geological Society. He also was a shareholder in the East India Company (Bowen 2006), which may explain how he managed to acquire the plants. Hume would have recognised the commercial value of the citrus trees and was probably instrumental in having them propagated.

In 1817 a representative mandarin branch was illustrated in *The Botanical Register* (Edwards 1817), where it was described thus:

▲ Seville sour orange is cultivated in the Mediterranean as a landscape tree as well as for its fruit and essential oils. Shown here in Inca, Majorca.

An entirely distinct species from the common China-Orange (*Citrus auran-tium*). In the large variety the fruit is deemed the most valuable of the genus, and called the Mandarin-Orange in virtue of its superiority. Both the large and small varieties were introduced by Sir Abraham Hume, by whom Mr. Edwards was favoured with the specimen from which the draw-ing was made. Native of Cochinchina [southern Vietnam]; cultivated at Canton. The fruit of the large sort sometimes measures [12.5 cm] 5 inches in diameter, and has a rind of deep saffron-colour. In *aurantium* the petiole of the leaf is edged by broad wings and of an obcordate form; in *nobilis* it is linear with an extremely narrow straight edging; in the former the fruit is nearly spherical, in the latter considerably depressed, so as to be of greater breadth than depth. The plant not having been yet cultivated in any of those countries from which we are supplied with oranges, the fruit has not found a place among the articles of commerce in this country. But we see no reason why it should not in the course of time.

Risso and Poiteau (1818–1822) appear to have been unaware of the man-darin when they first published their *Histoire naturelle des orangers*, a year after the publication of the painting in *The Botanical Register*. It was another 23 years before mandarins found their way to Italy, but by 1842 they were being extensively cultivated near Parma. The mandarin reached the United States between 1840 and 1850, after being introduced to Louisiana by the Italian consul to New Orleans (Hume 1957). Mandarins were probably introduced to Japan during the Tang Dynasty (618–906 A.D.) and eventually evolved, through human selection, into satsumas.

Lime

The lime probably originated in India and was taken to Persia and North Africa by the Arabs. It first appears in literature in the thirteenth century (Gallesio 1811) and was almost certainly taken to the West Indies in the late fifteenth or early sixteenth century.

◀ 'Tahiti' lime (*Citrus latifolia*) tolerates lower temperatures than the Mexican lime (*C. aurantifolia*).

Sweet Orange

For many years it was believed that the Portuguese had imported the sweet orange from India at the beginning of the sixteenth century. The Arabs controlled the monopoly in trade with India and this wasn't broken until 1509 when the Portuguese destroyed a combined Indian, Arab, and Egyptian fleet at the Battle of Diu. However, Christopher Columbus is known to have taken orange and lemon seeds to Hispaniola on his second voyage in 1493, which predates the Portuguese arrival in India in 1498. Citrus fruit eventually found their way to Florida (prior to 1579) and to South Carolina (prior to 1577).

The most likely story is that Genoese traders obtained the trees from Arabs after the Crusades. Oranges could have been obtained by the same clandestine method that was necessary for acquiring coffee beans. This was frequently a cloak-and-dagger affair and involved a considerable degree of personal risk. Whichever mechanism was responsible, sweet oranges were definitely being cultivated in Spain in the early sixteenth century and they may have arrived considerably earlier.

Sweet oranges probably reached the British Isles in the middle of the sixteenth century via Portugal. The two countries had had an alliance since 1373 and there was considerable trade between them. Indeed, sweet oranges were originally known as Portugal oranges, because they were first grown in that country.

One of the most colourful characters in British history is the London actress Nell (Eleanor) Gwynne (1650–1687). Nell is most famous for being one of King Charles the Second's mistresses, but started her life as an orange girl at the Theatre Royal in Drury Lane, London, when she was a teenager.

Oranges were obviously popular in Restoration London and the famous nursery rhyme 'Oranges and Lemons', which appears at the beginning of this book, is thought to have appeared at about this time. The rhyme is still popular with children and mentions six London churches, including St Clements. The final verse is rather gruesome, but this hasn't reduced the rhyme's popularity in our politically correct times.

The St Clements drink is an interesting concoction of cream, lemons, oranges, gelatine, Grand Marnier, and sugar. There are also St Clements cheesecakes, pastries, and mousses—all of which are made with lemons and oranges.

Grapefruit

Pummelos were known as Adam's apple during the Middle Ages and almost certainly originated in Indochina, like most citrus fruit. It seems likely these fruits were hybrids rather than the true pummelo. Giovanni Ferrari illustrated several cultivars in his famous book *Hesperides*, which was published in 1646.

Pummelos have long been cultivated in the Far East and there are many cultivars. They are also known as the shaddock, after Captain Phillip Shaddock, the commander of a ship belonging to the British East India Company, who took the seed to Barbados in the latter part of the seventeenth century (Sloane 1707–1726).

Grapefruit originated in the West Indies and is thought to be a natural hybrid between a pummelo and a sweet orange. The origin of the name

‘Marsh’ is the most widely grown grapefruit cultivar and provides most of the world's grapefruit juice.

▲ ‘Duncan’ is the granddad of all existing grapefruit cultivars, and all other grapefruit can trace their ancestry to this plant.

‘grapefruit’ is uncertain, but it could refer to the clusters of flowers or the way that the fruit hang on the tree. The fruit was slow in achieving popularity, and commercial production only started in Florida during the 1880s. The trend since the 1950s has been to develop seedless cultivars and darker pigmented grapefruit, such as ‘Star Ruby’. ‘Marsh’ grapefruit was found in 1860 and is still the most widely grown cultivar.

The Arrival of the Orangery

It would be impossible to write a book about citrus trees and not refer to the architectural phenomenon of the orangery. In Britain, orangeries are often one of the most attractive features of a country house and considerable amounts of money were spent on their construction. Orangeries were highly fashionable and probably built as a status symbol as well as for growing citrus fruit. They were the eighteenth-century equivalent of having an expensive car on the front drive!

The first orangeries were temporary structures that could be erected around citrus trees to protect them from frost. Later these structures were provided with wheels that allowed them to be moved away in the spring and placed into storage. The first purpose-built orangery was erected in Padua in the middle of the sixteenth century.

Sir Francis Carew (1530–1611) of Beddington, Surrey (now situated in the Borough of Sutton, London), has a good claim for being the first person to build an orangery in the British Isles. His was not a permanent building, but rather a temporary structure that protected his orange orchard. Most British gardeners will be amazed to discover that someone was crazy enough to establish a citrus orchard in England's relatively cold climate, where frosts are common throughout the winter. However, Carew's orchard appears to have been a great success and Queen Elizabeth the First is recorded as having tasted cherries there in 1599 (Lysons 1792).

Sir Francis is recorded as having purchased some lemon trees from Paris in 1562 and is said to have raised his orange trees from seed supplied by Sir Walter Raleigh, although other authors claim that Carew acquired them from Italy. Unfortunately, we have no way of knowing whether Sir Francis grew sour or sweet oranges, but it was most likely the former. The trees were grown in the ground and protected in the winter by a wooden shelter, with heating provided by two iron stoves. The shelter appears to have been a substantial structure with the upright posts left in the ground throughout the year and only the roof being erected in the autumn (Woods and Warren 1996). The orchard survived until the Great Frost of 1739–40.

John Evelyn, the English diarist and garden designer, visited the old house on 27 September 1658, during the latter years of Oliver Cromwell's Commonwealth, and made the following note in his diary:

> To Beddington, that ancient seat of the Carews, a fine old hall, but a scambling (sic) house, famous for the first orange-garden in England, being now over-grown trees, planted in the ground, and secured in winter with a wooden Tabernacle and stoves.

Queen Henrietta Maria, wife of the ill-fated King Charles the First of England, had two collections of citrus trees, the largest being kept in an orange house at Wimbledon Manor House. When the king was executed in 1649, Parliament carried out a valuation of his assets. In addition to 42 large orange trees, there were also lemons and pomegranates, worth an astonishing £558. This was an extremely large amount of money in the middle of the seventeenth century (Lysons 1792).

In France, the orangery at the Palace of the Louvre, in Paris, was built

◁ Citrus trees were an important feature of eighteenth-century gardens. They were placed outside in the spring and returned to the orangery in the autumn.

▷ The orangery at Mount Edgcumbe Country Park in Cornwall, England, was established in 1760. Very few orangeries are now used for their original purpose. The majority are used as restaurants or as a venue for wedding receptions.

in 1617 and inspired many others. André Le Nôtre, gardener to King Louis XIV of France, commenced the construction of an orange garden at the royal Palace of Versailles in 1661. The famous orangery was started in 1663 and was built into the side of a south-facing hill. This location protected the building from cold northerly winds and ensured that it received the maximum amount of light during the winter months. The citrus trees were planted in wooden boxes, which are still called Versailles containers or Versailles planters. The building spawned many imitators throughout Europe, and monarchs were soon building orangeries in emulation of the one at Versailles. It is still the largest orangery in existence and approximately a thousand citrus trees are overwintered in it.

Orangeries vary considerably in scale, but most share the same basic design. The typical orangery faces towards the south or southeast and has very tall windows that extend from floor level to just below the architrave. This placement ensures that the trees receive the maximum amount of light during the winter months and allows light to reflect off the rear wall. The rear wall was usually constructed from solid brick and heated by a furnace at the rear of the building.

Most orangeries have a very large door at the end or rear of the building, which allowed the trees to be moved indoors when there was a risk of frost. Moving the plants was a major undertaking because the trees were often very large and heavy, and forklift trucks were not available in the eighteenth century. Mature citrus trees often measured 4 metres (13 ft.) or more high and had a similar spread. The trees were kept within bounds by pruning, but the main doors to the orangery had to be large enough to accommodate them. Some orangeries, such as that at Kensington Palace in London, were provided with a stone terrace, which allowed the citrus trees to be moved more easily.

The largest orangery ever built in the British Isles is at Margam, near Swansea, in South Wales. It was started in 1768 and is 83 metres (275 ft.) long. This gigantic building is now used for wedding receptions, but in its heyday was home to huge citrus trees measuring up to 6 metres (20 ft.) high and 5.5 metres (18 ft.) across.

The citrus trees at Hampton Court Palace, in Surrey, were planted in wooden tubs with handles. When the trees were finally in the orangery, they were placed as close as possible to the front windows, so that they received the maximum amount of light. Early orangeries were permanently glazed, but later ones were built with windows that could be opened during mild weather. This enabled the trees to become acclimatised to the exterior air and greatly reduced the amount of condensation within the building.

Some orangeries, such as the one at Hanbury Hall in Worcestershire, were kept warm by heating the rear wall, while others, such as that at Avington Park in Hampshire, used a hypocaust beneath the floor.

The orangery at Kensington Palace in London was designed by Sir Christopher Wren and built for Queen Anne in 1704. It is a very elegant, brick-built structure with a Portland Stone terrace and carved cornice. It is one of the earliest orangeries to survive in the British Isles.

Unfortunately, most orangeries suffered from serious condensation, which eventually led to dry rot and other structural problems. This was the fate of the famous orangery at the Royal Botanic Gardens Kew, which was built in 1761 for Augusta, the Dowager Princess of Wales. The Kew orangery has been restored on several occasions but, like so many others, is currently used as a restaurant.

▲ Approximately one dozen mature citrus trees can be found in the Victorian glasshouse at Birmingham Botanical Gardens, in England.

◀ Citrus trees produce masses of highly fragrant flowers.

▶ 'Golden Special' blossom. The stamens of most citrus flowers are usually fused into groups of three or more.

3 Botany and Taxonomy

Citrus trees are attractive evergreen trees with dark green glossy foliage and edible, brightly coloured fruit. In the spring they produce masses of highly fragrant flowers, whose scent permeates the immediate area. The plants have a very complex history, which has only recently been revealed by chemical taxonomy and gene sequencing. The genus *Citrus* is endemic to tropical and subtropical parts of Southeast Asia.

Commercial citrus range from shrubs to medium-sized trees and have dense evergreen foliage. The majority are very vigorous and, depending upon the variety, can grow to a height of between 5 and 10 metres (16–33 ft.). Citrus trees are vulnerable to several diseases and physiological disorders and to counter this they are usually grafted onto a rootstock, which may also have a dwarfing effect upon the tree. Rootstocks are rarely completely compatible and the position of the graft union can still be seen in most grafted trees. The sour orange (*Citrus aurantium*) is a rare example of a citrus plant that can be grown on its own roots. The rootstock also has a major effect on the quality of citrus fruit and its ability to withstand environmental factors, such as cold, wet, alkalinity, and saline conditions.

Citrus leaves appear to be very simple, consisting of a single leaf and a petiole. They are, in reality, a reduced compound leaf, with only the terminal leaflet and its petiole remaining. Some citrus relatives, such as the genus *Citropsis*, have a compound trifoliate or pinnate leaf, while the trifoliate leaf form still occurs in *Poncirus trifoliata* (Spiegel-Roy and Goldschmidt 1996).

The leaves of many citrus have a winged petiole, and in some species (such as *Citrus hystrix*) this can be as large as the lamina of the leaf. The petiole wings are green and capable of photosynthesis. Thorns are often present above the leaf bud and can sometimes inflict a painful wound. They are particularly conspicuous in lemons, and this factor should be borne in mind when positioning trees close to a path. Young stems are occasionally triangular in cross-section and have a ridge below the base of the petiole. The stems gradually become round as the tree matures and secondary thickening takes place.

Cultivated citrus trees can live for a hundred years or more and will still be productive, but they are rarely kept this long in a commercial orchard. There are many examples of older trees, but in most cases the original trunks have rotted away and have been replaced by new growth from the base.

Floral Structure

Citrus flowers are small, but exude a wonderful fragrance that is capable of filling an entire room. The flowers have five sepals and petals, but the former are relatively inconspicuous and fused into a cup-shaped calyx. The sepals have pointed tips and often survive on the mature fruit. There are between four and eight petals, but usually five, and these are covered with conspicuous oil glands. Inside the petals is a ring of stamens that are fused at the base and arranged in groups of three or more around the style. At the base of the style is the ovary, which eventually matures into the fruit. The ovary has several carpels, each of which will develop into a fruit segment.

Citrus fruit are a special type of berry called a hesperidium. The well-known segments are derived from the carpels of the immature fruit and are filled with juice vesicles (juice sacs). The vesicles are derived from small papillae, which develop as outgrowths from the carpel wall. The papillae eventually grow so that they completely fill the interior of the carpel.

In navel oranges, a second set of carpels forms within the ovary, but does not develop into a complete fruit. Navels occur occasionally in other citrus cultivars, but they are invariably present in navel sweet oranges, such as the economically important 'Washington'. Navel oranges usually have malformed ovules and rarely produce any seeds. In some cases a second navel will be formed in the fruit, creating a tier.

The peel of a citrus fruit is composed of three layers. The outermost layer is called the epicarp and consists of a few layers of heavily cutinised cells, which protect the fruit from water loss. Beneath the epicarp is the hypoderm, which consists of several layers of thick-walled cells filled with pigmented plastids. There is no obvious boundary between the inner and outer mesocarps, which lie under the epicarp. The oil glands are embedded in the outer mesocarp, which is composed of thin-walled, pigmented

▶ Many citrus fruit look very similar on the surface, but differ internally. Shown here, top row left to right, are 'Tarocco' blood orange, Seville orange; middle row 'Lane Late' navel orange, 'Shamouti' orange; bottom row 'Valencia' orange, and 'Ortanique' mandarin.

cells. Beneath the outer mesocarp is the inner, which consists of numerous layers of colourless, elongated cells. This layer is spongy and protects the fruit from physical damage. When a fruit is peeled, it reveals a net of soft, colourless tissue. These are the vascular bundles, which connect the skin of the fruit to the central axis of the ovary. In some citrus the meso-carp separates from the carpels (or fruit segments) and leaves a gap. This often occurs in mandarins.

Oil glands are a very conspicuous feature of citrus plants and cover the entire flower and the skin of the mature fruit. When mature the oil glands are filled with highly aromatic oil, which has several commercial uses, including perfume.

Citrus trees will usually produce far more fruit than a tree can bear. The tree will often shed a large number of young fruit, which fall on the ground. This natural process ensures that the plant doesn't carry too much fruit. Young citrus trees are so productive that there is always a risk that the weight of the fruit will tear away a limb and cause permanent and sometimes fatal damage to the tree. Excessive fruit should be removed to make certain that this does not happen.

Breeding

While most of the older types of citrus have arisen following natural hybrid-isation between the different species and cultivars, the majority of modern cultivars have been produced through bud mutation. In this natural process a local genetic change in the bud produces a shoot that is genetically different from its parent. The change may only involve one or two genes,

but it may be sufficient to produce better flavour or cold tolerance. If the bud is removed and grafted onto a suitable rootstock, it can be used to produce a new plant that may be superior to its parent. Unfortunately, many of these new plants fail to live up to their initial promise and are discarded. There have been occasions in the past where a promising new cultivar has been propagated and planted in commercial orchards, only to find that it has some undesirable trait. This can result in a serious financial loss, and most modern cultivars are therefore extensively trialled before they are made available for commercial sale.

The asexual process of apomixis is also quite common in citrus, and seeds often have more than one embryo. Only one of these embryos is the result of sexual reproduction, while the others are often genetically identical to the parent and referred to as nucellar embryos. If the seed germinates, there is a strong chance that the resulting plant will be genetically identical to its parent—in other words, a clone. Occasionally, the nucellar seedlings differ very slightly from their parent and may be worth propagating as new cultivars. 'Frost Lisbon' lemon, a nucellar selection of the original 'Lisbon' lemon, is one example. Nucellar seedlings can also be used to produce virus-free plants.

More recently scientists have created new cultivars by irradiating seeds or budwood. The treatment increases the chances of a mutation occurring, but can introduce poor characteristics as well as good. One of the best examples of this is the 'Star Ruby' grapefruit, which was produced by irradiating the 'Hudson' grapefruit seed. 'Star Ruby' is generally speaking a very good variety, with large, juicy, sweet fruit and a darker colour than most other pigmented grapefruit. Unfortunately, experience has shown that it is less vigorous than other cultivars and is very sensitive to herbicides.

Several factors determine whether a cultivar will be a commercial success. Harvesting time is obviously important, because an early ripening cultivar will provide fruit that can be sold before the main crop and will usually sell for a higher price.

Another factor is how long the fruit can be left on the tree. Mature fruit start to deteriorate as soon as they are removed from the tree, but will normally remain in good condition if they are left on the tree. This characteristic allows the crop to be sold over a longer period, which in turn provides an income over a longer time. 'Valencia' orange, for example, will remain in good condition for several months if it is left on the tree, while 'Thomson' navel deteriorates quickly. Ageing fruit gradually shrinks, the skin becomes wrinkled, and the colour dull, so cultivars with better keeping qualities are preferred.

Some cultivars fall from favour because a plant that produces fewer seeds or easier-to-peel fruit supersedes them. Ironically, these are usually obtained as a bud mutation from the original tree. Today there are three main trends in citrus breeding: to produce cultivars that can be harvested earlier and over a longer period of time; to develop hybrids that will produce fruit in a cooler climate; and to breed seedless, easy-to-peel cultivars.

Taxonomy

The genus *Citrus* has proved to be somewhat of a nightmare for plant taxonomists. Probably the original ancestral species were geographically separated from one another, and as a consequence, no barrier to cross-pollination ever evolved. However, as soon as these species started to be cultivated, they were planted close to one another and were able to freely hybridise. There are now many hybrids in existence and it is almost impossible to unravel the parentage of each. Citrus trees also produce spontaneous bud or limb mutations and, when these are propagated, they add to the gene pool.

The ancient civilisations of Indochina must have grown citrus plants and this is probably where many of the modern species arose. Research suggests that there were originally five ancestral *Citrus* species, two of which have probably become extinct. Indochina is usually considered to be the countries to the east of India and south of China. This area now includes the modern states of Cambodia, Laos, Malaysia, Myanmar (Burma), Thailand, and Vietnam. Cultivation probably extended into India and China and as far south as Indonesia.

To make matters worse, it seems likely that the names of cultivars have been muddled up when the plants have been transported around the world. 'Bearss' lime is a perfect example of this. Some people consider that 'Bearss' lime is identical to 'Tahiti' lime, while others believe it is different. It really depends upon where the original specimens originated and whether they themselves were true to name. The problem even extends to such well-known plants as 'Washington' navel. For many years it was believed that this plant originated from Brazil, when in reality it seems to have come from Spain. Several plants that appear identical to 'Washington' navel have been grown in different parts of the world.

Two main classifications of the genus *Citrus* are currently in use. The Japanese botanist Tyôzaburô Tanaka described approximately 160 species in the early twentieth century and would now be described as a 'splitter'. The various species are described in eight scientific papers published between 1918 and 1937 and cited by Webber and Batchelor (1943) in volume one of *The Citrus Industry*. Many of Tanaka's species are still recognised, but the overall scheme is cumbersome and not supported by modern genetic research. For example, Tanaka divided the mandarins into *C. clementina* (clementines), *C. deliciosa* (temple mandarin), *C. nobilis* (king mandarin), *C. reshni* ('Cleopatra' mandarin), *C. tangerina* (tangerines), and *C. unshiu* (satsumas). There are in reality very few morphological differences between these plants and it is consequently difficult to justify maintaining them as independent species. However, the names are already well entrenched in horticulture and it may be difficult to revert to the new, more natural system.

Walter Swingle (1943), an American scientist working for the U.S. Department of Agriculture, recognised only sixteen species and would now be regarded as a 'lumper'. His coverage of the genus *Citrus* is only a small part of a much larger classification of the orange subfamily Aurantioideae—a truly mammoth undertaking. Swingle considered that all of Tanaka's mandarins were one species (*C. reticulata*). He placed all of the cultivated forms of *Citrus* in subgenus *Eucitrus*, which was distinguished by having lateral sepal bundles fused with the petal midrib. He placed the remaining species in subgenus *Papeda*; only one of these species (*C. hystrix*) is of any commercial significance. Swingle's classification is, on the whole, supported by recent genetic and chemical studies (see following). A simplified version of his classification is shown here:

Subgenus *Eucitrus*
    Citrus tachibana (Tachibana orange)
    Citrus limon (lemon)
    Citrus reticulata (mandarin)
    Citrus indica (Indian wild orange)
    Citrus grandis (pummelo—now *C. maxima*)
    Citrus paradisi (grapefruit)
    Citrus aurantifolia (lime)
    Citrus sinensis (sweet orange)
    Citrus aurantium (sour orange)
Subgenus *Papeda*
    Citrus ichangensis (Ichang papeda)
    Citrus latipes (Khasi papeda)
    Citrus micrantha (small-flowered papeda)
    Citrus celebica (Celebes papeda)
    Citrus macroptera (Melanesian papeda)
    Citrus hystrix (Thai lime)

Citrus are very similar from a morphological point of view, and Mabberley (1997) considered that it was only their commercial importance that led to so many species being described. While the number of morphological differences between citrus is limited, several chemicals in citrus have proved to have taxonomic value. Scora and Kumamoto (1983) have used these to show that there are in fact only four wild species of *Citrus*: the pummelo (*C. maxima*), the citron (*C. medica*), the mandarin (*C. reticulata*), and a tropical species, *C. halimii*. All of the cultivated varieties of *Citrus* are now believed to have arisen by hybridisation between the first three of these species and two others that are now extinct. *Citrus halimii* was only discovered recently (Stone et al. 1973) and is endemic to Malaya and Thailand.

    Mabberley (1998) consequently suggested that subgenus *Eucitrus* should be divided into three species—*Citrus medica*, *C. maxima*, and *C. reticulata*—and that the cultivars were best placed in hybrid groups within these species. Hybrid species are prefixed with the symbol ×, as in *C. ×limon*.

In some cases the parentage of certain cultivars, such as 'Meyer' lemon', is unknown and these are represented by the genus name followed by the cultivar name, as in C. 'Meyer'. The new classification is as follows:

Citrus medica (citron)
   Citrus ×*limon* (lemons)
   Citrus ×*jambhiri* (rough lemons)
Citrus maxima (pummelo)
   Citrus ×*aurantifolia* (limes)
   Citrus ×*aurantium* (oranges and grapefruits)
Citrus reticulata (tangerines, satsumas, clementines)

While Mabberley's classification may seem like a rather radical solution, it is supported by a comparison of gene sequencing within these species. *Citrus medica*, however, appears to be very different from the other species in the genus (Araújo et al. 2003). This is unfortunate as *C. medica* is currently the type species for the genus and all descriptions of *Citrus* are based upon it. The research by Araújo and colleagues has also shown that there is very little difference between the species in the two subgenera *Papeda* and *Eucitrus*.

Pang et al. (2007) have studied the phylogeny of the genus using DNA from citrus leaves. They found that *Citrus maxima*, *C. medica*, and *C. reticulata* formed three distinct clusters and that there was therefore good justification in recognising them as the ancestral species for all of the cultivated varieties, if not for the other species in the genus.

Swingle's classification is still the most widely used, partly because it is more manageable than Tanaka's. Tanaka's classification included 160 species, such as *Citrus bergamia* and *C. jambhiri*, which were not accepted by Swingle. The following list compares selected citrus names used by Tanaka and Swingle:

Tanaka's names	Swingle's names
Citrus bergamia	*Citrus aurantifolia*
Citrus canaliculata	*Citrus aurantium*
Citrus clementina	*Citrus reticulata*
Citrus deliciosa	*Citrus reticulata*
Citrus halimii	No equivalent name
Citrus jambhiri	*Citrus limon*

Citrus latifolia	*Citrus aurantifolia*
Citrus limetta	*Citrus limon*
Citrus limonia	*Citrus limon*
Citrus lumia	*Citrus limon*
Citrus macrophylla	*Citrus aurantifolia*
Citrus meyeri	*Citrus limon*
Citrus myrtifolia	*Citrus aurantium*
Citrus nobilis	*Citrus reticulata*
Citrus peretta	*Citrus limon*
Citrus pyriformis	*Citrus limon*
Citrus unshiu	*Citrus reticulata*

It would be impossible to untangle the different names from the two classification systems within the confines of this book. I have therefore used the names as they are most widely used in horticulture.

It is often very difficult to determine whether two plant cultivars are identical and this is particularly so with citrus, where the differences between plants may be very subtle. The only way to be certain is to obtain specimens that have a known provenance and to grow them in identical conditions. In the case of citrus this takes considerable space and can only be achieved by large institutions such as the University of California, Riverside.

Terminology

For cultivars names I have followed *Citrus of the World* (Cottin 2002), published by the National Institute of Agricultural Research (INRA) and the Centre of International Co-operation and Research on Agricultural Development (CIRAD) in France. Their list of synonyms includes most of the known cultivars and extends to 62 pages in length, but has the advantage of being available as a PDF document on the Internet. Cultivar names are often spelt differently from place to place and handwritten labels are frequently misread.

▲ A lemon orchard in Majorca, Spain

4 Economic Uses of Citrus Fruit

Citrus are by far the most important fruit crop in the world and exceed the total production of all other fruit such as apples, cherries, peaches, and plums. According to United Nations statistics, the total world production of citrus fruit in 2004–05 was 94.8 million, including 59 million tons of oranges, 19 million tons of tangerines (mandarins), 11.7 million tons of lemons and limes, and almost 5 million tons of grapefruit (FAO 2006). The largest producer of those fruit was Brazil (18.9 million tons), followed by China (15.2 million tons) and the United States (10.5 million tons). Brazil and the United States lead the world in the production of oranges, Japan and Spain produce the majority of mandarins, Mexico and Spain the largest number of lemons and limes, and China and the United States grow the highest number of grapefruit.

In 2005 the citrus-producing countries of the world exported 2.3 million tons of concentrated orange juice, 119,600 tons of concentrated lemon juice, and 242,200 tons of grapefruit juice. To this can be added 1.8 million tons of single-strength orange juice, 59,200 tons of lemon juice, and 160,300 tons of grapefruit juice.

The mandarin has been growing in popularity since the 1950s, partly because the fruit are so much easier to peel than many oranges. In 1957 Harold Hume stated:

> It must be borne in mind however, that the mandarin fruit is essentially a fancy fruit and as such commands a fancy price in its season, but it would be useless to attempt to place it on the same production level with the sweet orange as a staple fruit.

The current production levels in Spain suggest that Hume was wrong in his assumption.

Commercial Uses of Citrus

Citrus oil is one the most effective degreasants known to mankind and is capable of removing oil, chewing gum, tar, ink, soap, and adhesives. The effective ingredient is the terpene d-limonene, which is biodegradable and used at a concentration of between 5 and 15 percent in water. It is non-poisonous, but so effective at removing grease that it can be used to clean car engines, bathrooms, and even dirty barbeques.

Oil of neroli is highly aromatic and extracted from the flowers of the sour orange (*Citrus aurantium*). According to tradition, it was first introduced in the seventeenth century when Anna Maria de la Tremoille de Noirmutier, wife of Flavio Orsini, Prince of Nerola, started to use it as a perfume. The oil is an important component of many modern perfumes and is used in eau de cologne.

Citrus oil contains many highly volatile chemicals, which will evaporate if the temperature is too high. Considerable care must be taken when the flowers are harvested. The flower buds are collected when they first open in the morning and before the ambient temperature is too high. The main producers are France and Tunisia, but it is also produced in several other countries around the Mediterranean Sea. The oil is extracted from the flowers by using steam distillation. It takes almost 1000 kilograms (2200 lbs) of raw material to produce 1 kilogram (2.2 lbs) of neroli oil.

Eau de Cologne is technically a 'toilet water' because it contains less essential oil than a true perfume. It is a blend of neroli oil, bergamot, rosemary, lime, orange, lavender, and jasmine oils, dissolved in ethanol. Jean Maria Farina invented the original perfume in 1709, while he was in Cologne. The original formula is secret, but the perfume became so popular that many others copied the idea. The original eau de cologne is still called '4711', after the number of the house in Cologne, where it was created.

Oil of petitgrain was originally distilled from the small unripe fruits of sour orange, but is now made from the leaves and smallest branches of the tree. The original process was very wasteful, because it removed fruit that could be used for other purposes. The material is collected from July to September and extracted by using the cold press process, which preserves the highly volatile oils. Several countries produce the oil, but the highest-quality oil is produced in France and Italy.

Citrus fruit have long been used as a flavouring for soft drinks, though most commercial drinks are carbonated and use artificial flavouring.

Lemons and limes are used in a range of alcoholic drinks, while mixing orange juice with champagne makes Buck's Fizz. Lemon juice is widely used in cookery and can be used to stop apples from turning brown after they have been cut.

Curaçao liqueur was first invented on the island of the same name and is flavoured with the peel of 'Laraha', a locally grown form of sour orange (*Citrus aurantium*). 'Laraha' grows wild on the island of Curaçao and is presumed to have grown from the discarded seeds of imported Seville oranges. The peel is dried in the sun and then soaked in alcohol. After a few days the peel is removed and spices are added to provide the liqueur with its distinctive flavour. There are several different colours of Curaçao, including the famous blue, plus white, orange, red, and green. The drink is made in several other countries, apart from Curaçao.

Large quantities of 'Valencia' oranges are used to produce frozen concentrated orange juice (FCOJ). The juice is extracted by machine and the excess water removed by heating. The juice can be concentrated to as much as seven times its normal concentration. This greatly reduces transport costs and allows the juice to be exported around the world. Frozen juice is a major commodity on world markets and can be stored for several years. The pulp that remains after the juice is extracted is squeezed in a machine to remove any remaining liquid. The liquid is used to make citrus molasses, which can be fermented to produce alcohol or added to the peel and used to produce pellets for animal feed. Navel oranges cannot be used to produce fruit juice because they contain a bitter-tasting chemical called limonin.

There is also a growing demand for non-concentrated orange juice (known commercially as 'not-from-concentrate orange juice' or NFC). NFC is pasteurised by flash heating and can be stored for up to a year. It is cheaper than freshly squeezed orange juice, but costs more to transport than FCOJ because it contains the original concentration of water.

Bergamot oil is extracted from the peel of *Citrus bergamia* and used in a wide range of perfumes. The highest quality bergamot oil comes from the province of Calabria, in southern Italy, but smaller amounts are also cultivated in Argentina, Brazil, and the Ivory Coast. The highest quality oil is obtained by cold pressing. Oil of bergamot has many uses: as an antiseptic, to make marmalade, to flavour candy, and even as an ingredient of soaps and creams.

◀ Bergamot (*Citrus bergamia*) is grown for its highly aromatic oil used in perfume and to flavour Earl Grey tea.

Earl Grey is an up-market blend of black tea and one of the more unusual uses of citrus fruit. The tea was first blended in the 1830s and is named after Charles, the second Earl Grey, who was prime minister of the United Kingdom from 1830 to 1834. The dried tea is sprayed with bergamot oil and has a more delicate flavour than most blended black teas. Twinings of London, which was established in 1706, claims to have invented Earl Grey tea, but this claim is disputed by Jacksons of Piccadilly, another famous tea-blender. The former also produces a Lady Grey tea, which is flavoured with Seville oranges, lemon, and bergamot.

Citrus fruit also yield a large amount of pectin, which is used to thicken jellies and jams. A modified form of citrus pectin has shown promise as a treatment for cancer.

Grapefruit has several uses apart from that of a dessert fruit or as a source of juice. The raw oil is dark brown and very bitter, but after refining it can be used as an alternative to olive oil. The soft mesocarp yields the chemical naringin, which is used as a flavouring in bitter chocolate, while the peel contains large amounts of pectin.

Citrus in Cookery

Citrus hystrix is an important ingredient in Thai cuisine, where it is known as *makrud* or *makrut*, and its leaves (*bai makrud*) are used in many dishes, such as *Dtom Yum Gkoong* (hot and sour prawn soup) and *Gaeng Keow Wan Gai* (Thai green chicken curry). The leaves of *C. hystrix* have a very pungent taste, which can easily overwhelm the more subtle flavours in a dish. The midrib of the leaf should be removed and the remaining part cut

◀ The distinctive leaves of *Citrus hystrix* are used to flavour Thai food.

▶ Although the knobby fruit of *Citrus hystrix* are inedible, they yield oil with insecticidal properties that is useful as a hair shampoo, a bleaching agent during washing, and a natural air freshener.

into very thin slices. Fresh leaves can be shredded and used as a garnish in salads or sprinkled over curries. The leaves are very distinctive, with a large expanded petiole that is often as large as the true leaf. While fresh material is always preferable, the leaves can be kept frozen for up to a year. The fruit also yield oil that has insecticidal properties. The oil can be removed by steam distillation.

Lime juice is an essential ingredient of many alcoholic drinks, including margaritas. The fruit are extremely bitter, but they have an incredibly number of culinary uses. They are also used as a soft drink. In the late eighteenth century, sailors in the British Royal Navy were given West Indian limes to stop them from getting scurvy.

In North America, Key lime pie is synonymous with the Florida Keys, where the recipe was developed in the late nineteenth century. At that time there were no refrigerators and people had learnt to rely upon condensed milk, which is one of the main ingredients of the pie.

Key Lime Pie

Crust ingredients
220 g (6 oz) digestive biscuits, crushed
120 g (½ c) granulated sugar
60 g (2 oz) butter, melted

Filling ingredients
410 g (14 oz) condensed milk
120 ml (½ c) lime juice (about 5 limes)

Instructions
Mix the biscuit crumbs with the sugar and melted butter. Press the mixture into a 23-cm (9-in.) pie tin and bake in an oven for approximately 20 minutes at 200°C (39°F).

Mix the milk and lime juice. Then add the mixture to the baked and cooled pie base and place it in a refrigerator for an hour or so to set. The pie can be finished off with a whipped cream or meringue topping, depending upon taste. Garnish it with thin slices of lime before serving.

Marmalade is a popular conserve eaten on toasted bread. It is usually made from Seville oranges, but can also be made from grapefruit, lemon, lime, and other citrus fruit. The English word *marmalade* is probably derived from the Portuguese *marmelada*, a form of quince jam (Portuguese *marmelada* is still made from quince). King Henry the Eighth of England is recorded as having received a gift of marmalade in the early sixteenth century and it was probably made from quinces. Seville oranges usually have enough natural pectin to ensure that the marmalade sets properly, but commercial products usually have a lower amount of fruit and need gelling agents to ensure that they are solid.

The recipe that follows is one I have used to make marmalade several times. It was originally written by Delia Smith (www.deliasmith.com). Normal dessert oranges are unsuitable for making marmalade. For a little extra flavour, add a couple of dessert spoons of molasses or some whiskey.

Orange Marmalade

Ingredients
1.9 litres (8 c) water
900 g (2 lbs) Seville oranges
1 lemon
1.8 kg (4 lbs) granulated sugar

Supplies
Muslin cloth, 30-cm (12-in.) square
Short length of string
Funnel
6 glass jam jars, 350 ml (1 lb) each

Instructions
Sterilize the jars by placing them in the oven for 10 minutes at 200°C (390°F). Carefully remove them from the oven, placing them on a warm insulated surface (they may shatter if set on a cold surface).

Put the water in a large saucepan. Wash the fruit, slice them in two, then extract the juice and add it to the water. Cut the remaining fruit skins into quarters and then slice them carefully with a sharp knife. The thickness of the slices depends upon personal taste.

Collect all of the pith and seeds and place them in a piece of clean muslin fabric. Tie the muslin with a clean piece of string so that it forms a small bag and attach it to the handle of the saucepan so that it hangs in the water (the seeds and pith contain pectin, which makes the completed marmalade set).

Bring the water up to boiling point and let the marmalade mixture simmer for approximately 2 hours. Reduce the heat and remove the small muslin bag. The lemon and orange skins should be soft.

Now add the sugar gradually to the boiled fruit mixture, stirring continuously so that it dissolves. When the sugar is completely dissolved, turn up the heat until the marmalade mixture is boiling. Squeeze the contents of the muslin bags so that all of the juice falls into the mixture.

continued over

After 20 minutes remove the saucepan from the heat and pour a small amount of the marmalade mixture into a cold dish. Place the dish in the fridge and leave it to set. If the mixture does not set, heat the marmalade mixture for another 10 minutes until it does. If the marmalade still refuses to set, you can add some commercial pectin to the mixture, but this shouldn't be necessary.

Remove the saucepan from the heat and allow it to cool slightly. Remove any scum with a tablespoon and pour the contents of the saucepan into the sterilised glass jars using a clean funnel. Cover the marmalade with a paper disc and close the lid. Label the bottles when they are cold and keep them in a cool, dark place.

We now know that citrus fruit provide essential nutrients in our diets, especially vitamin C, but back in the seventeenth and eighteenth centuries, scurvy was a serious disease among sailors. Anyone living on land obtained enough vitamin C from fresh vegetables, but these were not available to sailors who spent months and often years at sea. Many died or suffered from serious illness during long voyages, and some sailors lost their teeth because of scurvy. The human body needs vitamin C to produce collagen, an important structural protein that is found in cartilage, tendons, bones, and teeth. Without vitamin C, the sailors suffered from liver spots, tooth loss, bleeding around the gums, and suppurating wounds. In 1747, James Lind, a Scottish surgeon in the Royal Navy, carried out an experiment on board the British warship HMS *Salisbury* to see if he could prove the cause of the disease. He gave some sailors cider, some seawater, some vinegar, and a final group lemons and oranges. The health of the latter improved so quickly that the link was immediately made, even though the reason for the improvement was less clear. Lind's findings were published in his book *A Treatise of the Scurvy* (1753).

In 1876 the Merchant Shipping Act was introduced in Britain, which made it mandatory for sailors in the Royal Navy and Merchant Navy to drink a ration of lime juice. In the same year Lauchlin Rose, a Scottish businessman, patented a new non-alcoholic drink made from sweetened lime juice. The drink is still sold as Rose's lime juice cordial. According to tradition, this is how the British became known as 'limeys' to Americans and Canadians.

Both the citron and its more extravagant offspring, 'Buddha's Hand' citron, can be used to perfume laundry and rooms. The fruit can be candied or grated and used in salads.

◁ 'Tahiti' lime fruit are deep green when young, but turn yellow-green and then yellow as they become fully ripe.

▷ 'Buddha's Hand' citron is one of the oddest fruit in existence and always attracts attention.

Grapefruit are mainly grown as a dessert fruit and for the manufacture of juice, but they can also be used to make a very pleasant marmalade. Red grapefruit can be used to make an excellent salad with sliced avocados.

Grapefruit and Avocado Salad

Ingredients
I avocado, peeled, pitted, and sliced lengthwise
I red grapefruit, peeled and segmented
Iceberg lettuce leaves
Walnuts
White grapes, sliced
Extra virgin olive oil
Wine vinegar
Black pepper, freshly ground

Instructions
Mix the grapefruit segments and avocado slices together and place on a bed of iceberg lettuce. Add a handful of walnuts and some sliced white grapes. Sprinkle with vinaigrette, composed of equal amounts of extra virgin olive oil and wine vinegar. Add freshly ground black pepper to taste.

Few fruit have played such an important role in cookery as the humble lemon. The familiar yellow fruit have found their way into numerous desserts, including cheesecake, mousse, meringue, soufflé, lemon curd, and sorbet. The list goes on and on. Not only is the juice valued, but also the zest of the fruit, which contains essentials oils.

Lemon juice is invaluable for cooking fish, and grilled plaice is usually accompanied by a slice of the fruit. The juice can also be used as a marinade, to prevent fresh fish from smelling and sliced apples from turning brown, and to make limoncello, a lemon-based liquor. Lemon juice is used to clean silverware and working surfaces in kitchens, as an insecticide and a hair lightener, and has many other nefarious uses.

The fruit makes a wonderful drink—lemonade—which has been drunk for over three centuries and is remarkably easy to make.

Lemonade

Ingredients
285 ml (1 c) water
285 ml (1 c) sugar
6 lemons, washed
1–1.5 litres (4–5 c) water

Instructions
Boil 285 ml (1 c) of water in a saucepan and then add an equal amount of sugar. Stir the water until all of the sugar is dissolved. After cooling the mixture, decant it into a jug. Remove the juice from the lemons, strain to remove any pips, and then add the juice to the jug of water. Dilute the mixture with up to 1.5 litres (5 c) of water and place the lemonade in a fridge for an hour or so to cool down. This will produce an extremely strong drink, which can be diluted to taste.

Kumquat fruit are quite tiny, but they have many culinary uses. Slice them up and use the slices as decoration on desserts or eat them whole, complete with the rind and any pips. They have plenty of natural pectin in the skin and can be use in preserves, candied, or in cooking. 'Calamondin' orange, probably a hybrid between a mandarin and a kumquat, has numerous uses, including a few rather bizarre ones. The fruit can be eaten whole, made into marmalade, candied, or frozen and used as ice cubes in alcoholic drinks.

Citrus Plants for Cookery

The following list of citrus trees should enable you to cater for most culinary situations, from Thai cuisine to the occasional batch of orange marmalade. The plants can be grown under cover in most cool climates, as long as they are provided with sufficient light.

Sweet orange (for eating)	'Washington' navel
Sweet orange (for juice and eating)	'Valencia'
Blood orange	'Tarocco'
Mandarin	'Owari' Satsuma
Mandarin	'Nules' clementine
Lemon	'Garey's Eureka' or 'Lisbon'
Lemon (hybrid)	'Improved Meyer'
New Zealand grapefruit	'Golden Special'
Lime	'Tahiti'
Thai lime	*Citrus hystrix*
Kumquat	'Nagami'
Sour orange (for marmalade)	Seville

While it is possible to grow grapefruit in a cool temperate climate, they are unlikely to produce edible fruit. A New Zealand grapefruit, such as 'Golden Special', looks very similar to true grapefruit and should ripen in a warm summer.

Flavour of Fruit

Most sweet oranges and mandarins look very similar and their external appearance provides few clues as to how they will taste when they have been peeled. Navel oranges are the mainstay of the dessert fruit market and 'Washington' navel is still the standard by which all others are judged. Its fruit are easy to peel, the segments are easy to separate, the juice is sweet, and the flavour is wonderful.

Citrus juice is a cocktail of many different chemicals including acids, starch, flavonoids, sugars, pigments, proteins, and vitamins. The balance of these chemicals depends upon the cultivar, the age of the fruit, and the conditions under which the fruit have been grown and stored. Young fruit have quite high starch levels, but this falls as they ripen and the starch is converted into sucrose.

Mandarins are even more variable than oranges and it is almost impossible to guess the eating qualities of a fruit from its external appearance. They vary in shape from spherical to oblate (shaped like a pumpkin) and obovoid (egg-shaped, with the narrow end pointing towards the stem). Deep orange fruit may appear ripe and should taste sweet, but in reality a slightly green Satsuma can taste sweeter than a bright orange-red unnamed mandarin. 'Valencia' fruit rarely turn orange in a tropical climate, remaining green with rather pale juice, while some navel oranges will turn green again if they are left on the tree for too long. The flavour is, however, usually unaffected and the fruit can still be used to make acceptable fruit juice.

The cultivar name is often the only way of judging how a citrus fruit will taste. Supermarkets often sell fruit with a generic label on the outside that simply says 'mandarin' or 'clementine'. The best-quality mandarins are usually available in the autumn or early winter, but by early spring the better cultivars have been sold and are replaced by their lesser brethren, whose taste may be sour or insipid. Citrus from countries in the Southern Hemisphere are usually available six months later. However, the name of the cultivar can often be found on the box in which the fruit were delivered. Just be prepared for some strange looks from the other people in the store!

A well-grown clementine, such as 'Nules', has a very pleasant flavour with a good balance of sweetness and acidity. Very sweet fruit can have a rather bland and unappealing flavour, while fruit with some acidity have a taste that approaches the complexity of a good quality wine. Some blood oranges, such as 'Tarocco', have a very complex flavour and the taste can linger in your mouth for an hour or more.

Citrus peel also varies in its aroma. Most commercial fruit are washed to remove pests, dirt, and fungus and then coated with a natural, but artificially refined wax. This process removes most of the aroma and then seals in the remaining scent with a waterproof coat. Organic fruit are not treated in this way and usually have a much stronger smell than conventionally produced fruit.

▲ 'Owari' fruit take some time to develop their characteristic colour but, like fruit of other satsumas, are sweet enough for eating when they are still partially green.

Freshly squeezed orange juice is far superior to that reconstituted from concentrate, but it is important to use the correct type of orange. 'Valencia' oranges are preferable to navels because the latter contain low concentrations of the very bitter-tasting chemical limonin. Commercially produced juices also include a number of naturally occurring chemicals from the peel that are absent from hand-squeezed juice.

Blood oranges are very popular in Italy, where farmers grow several different cultivars. The juice has a very distinctive flavour and, while it is popular in Italy, it is less widely drunk elsewhere. Some people are put off by the appearance of the internal segments.

Most plant species rely upon seeds for their long-term survival, but they are undesirable to most consumers and seedless fruit tend to command higher prices than those with seeds. Many citrus trees will only produce seeds if they are cross-pollinated by another compatible and genetically different plant, so pollen from the same cultivar will not produce viable seeds. Growers reduce the amount of cross-pollination by planting large blocks of a single cultivar. Bees usually pollinate the outer trees in an orchard and produce seedy fruit, but trees further in the orchard are likely to be seedless. Smaller growers cannot afford to plant on such an extensive scale and are more likely to produce seedy fruit.

Regardless of all the advances that have been made in plant breeding over the last century, a small number of old cultivars still dominate the citrus fruit industry. Among the oranges, 'Washington' navel (1870) and 'Valencia' (pre-1860) still hold sway, while the grapefruit trade is still dominated by 'Marsh', which was first discovered in 1860. One of the main reasons for this is that citrus trees can be grafted onto another rootstock. This has enabled growers to cope with a number of serious diseases such as phytophthora, exocortis, and citrus tristeza virus.

Because citrus trees in a container can become top heavy, buy pots with a broad base and fill the bottom of the pot with gravel to improve stability.

Citrus trees grow very well in terracotta pots, but the pots are prone to break if they fall over.

5 Soil and Nutrition

Three important decisions facing the home gardener of citrus plants involve choosing an appropriate compost, finding a suitable container, and selecting a balanced fertiliser.

Compost

The majority of citrus trees are purchased as containerised plants and will have been planted in a peat-based compost. Such compost provides an ideal growing medium for most plants, but my personal experience suggests that citrus grow better in a loam-based (soil-based) material, which is well aerated and provides good drainage.

If you choose to use a loam-based compost, it is a good idea to remove some of the existing peat-based compost from the root ball before re-potting the plant. Doing so will ensure that the roots penetrate the new compost rather than remain within the ball of old compost. Under no circumstances should you use unsterilised garden soil for potting up your plants. Such soil may harbour phytophthora or pathogenic nematodes.

Most British growers will use one of the John Innes (loam-based) composts, which were first formulated in the 1940s. They are made with seven parts of sterilised loam, three parts of peat, two parts of grit-sand, and different amounts of nutrients according to the purpose of the compost. John Innes No. 1 has one part of the fertiliser mixture, No. 2 has two parts, and No. 3 three. While the peat improves the structure and water-holding ability of the compost, it also increases the acidity, so most John Innes composts have ground limestone added to counteract this. Some citrus rootstocks, such as trifoliate orange, are lime-intolerant and it is therefore safer to use the recently introduced John Innes ericaceous compost, which does not include any lime.

In practice, most people seem to have little problem using John Innes

No. 2 or 3 for their citrus, but if plants growing in such a compost start to show signs of chlorosis, the excess lime can be counteracted by adding yellow flowers of sulphur. Sulphur is not water-soluble but will gradually oxidise and counter the effects of the lime. The pH of recently packed organic compost ranges from 5.5 to 6.0, but loam-based compost is more alkaline with a pH between 6.0 and 7.0. Shortly after the compost is used, the pH rises slightly because of natural chemical processes. It then falls as the organic nitrogen is converted into organic compounds.

While loam-based composts have many advantages, they are very heavy and containers filled with such composts are not easily moved, a factor that should be borne in mind when planning a collection. It is very tempting to keep potting-on your plants, but in reality most mature citrus trees do well in a 38-centimetre (15-in.) pot. It is only practical to use larger pots if you live a mild climate where the plants can be left outside throughout the year or if you have access to a forklift truck. Half-barrels are cheap and relatively decorative, but they will become a permanent fixture when they have been filled with soil. Mature plants do not need to be re-potted and it is only necessary to remove the top few centimetres of compost every couple of years and replace it with fresh. This practice helps to remove any build-up of minerals and replaces compost that may have been washed out during watering.

In recent years there has been a lot of pressure from environmental groups to reduce the use of peat-based composts. Peat is usually obtained from a raised bog, an increasingly rare habitat that developed after the last ice age. In ideal conditions a peat bog can grow at about 15 millimetres (5/8 in.) per year, but this is rarely achieved and most raised bogs have already been exploited on an industrial scale. The most important component of peat from a horticultural perspective is sphagnum moss, a lower plant with an amazing ability to absorb water and nutrients. The cells of sphagnum moss are full of tiny holes and act like a sponge. Manufacturers have tried very hard to find a substitute for peat, but unfortunately very few of them have proved to be as good as the traditional composts.

Most peat-free composts are made from coir fibre, composted green waste, or bark. These materials can be used successfully, but it is important to check the pH from time to time, as the media have a tendency to oxidise and become too acidic. The pH can be corrected by adding ground limestone, but in reality it is often easier to re-pot the plant in fresh compost than to resort to 'bucket chemistry'. The best pH for growing citrus is between 6.0 and 7.0. Peat-free composts do not retain as much water as those based on peat, and plants may need watering more frequently.

Choosing a Suitable Pot

Citrus definitely prefer to be grown in a terracotta pot. Because terracotta is porous, it not only allows the roots to breathe but also reduces the risk of the compost becoming waterlogged. When tapped, a wet terracotta pot will make a different sound than a dry one, and this difference, together with the darker colour of a wet pot, can be used to determine whether or not the plant needs watering.

The main disadvantage of terracotta is its weight, and some people will have no option other than to use plastic pots. Terracotta pots also vary considerably in quality so it is a good idea to spend as much as you can on them. Cheap, machine-made pots are often a false economy because they invariably crack if the plant falls over on a windy day or they fail after a slight frost. The broken terracotta is extremely sharp and should be treated with care.

If a terracotta pot is going to be placed on a very smooth surface, it is a good idea to raise it above the ground by using terracotta feet. This is a very effective way to ensure that the water can drain away properly, although raising the pots makes them less stable in windy weather.

Containerised citrus are vulnerable to damage in high winds, particularly if they have a large amount of foliage. The most stable specimens are those planted in soil-based compost and terracotta pots, but the latter are likely to crack if they are knocked over by high winds. To prevent this from happening, only partly fill the pot with compost; then top-dress the compost with at least 2.5 centimetres (1 in.) of horticultural grit. The grit performs two functions: it prevents weeds from growing on the compost and, because it is much heavier than the planting medium, it keeps the pot firmly on the ground during inclement weather. The grit can be removed during the winter to reduce the weight of the pot and make it easier to move.

If weight of the container is an issue, it is more sensible to use organic composts and plastic containers. Plastic pots vary considerable in quality and some manufacturers have successfully mimicked the appearance of terracotta. Avoid using a pot that has a lip on the inside because this will make it extremely difficult to remove the tree when it needs to be re-potted. It is also a good idea to use a pot with a broad base as it is far more stable

Plastic pots are much lighter than terracotta pots.

Holes in a pot can be used to improve drainage.

Considerable care needs to be taken when moving citrus trees. Potted citrus plants are very heavy.

than a comparable pot with a narrow base and is less likely to be blown over in stormy weather. Gravel can be added to the bottom of the pot to reduce the chances of it being blown over in a strong wind.

Whichever type of pot you use, make sure that it has a large, central hole in the bottom, which is big enough to allow water to drain out. To improve drainage, place a quantity of broken terracotta pot inside the container before you fill it up with compost, making sure that the pieces aren't obscuring the drainage hole.

One of the biggest mistakes is to over-pot a citrus tree. Always use the next pot size up rather than planting citrus in a larger pot in the hope that it will grow faster—it won't.

I have moved out of a house on several occasions and my citrus trees have always come with me. It is important to realise that a mature citrus tree is very heavy, particularly if it is in a terracotta pot. In most cases you will need a box van with a tail lift. The heaviest plants should be placed at the front of the vehicle, with the lighter ones at the rear. It is important to fill the empty space with something that will stop the load from moving around. Finally make sure that you lock the rear door.

Fertiliser

Most cultivated plants will grow well in a pot filled with good-quality compost and will only need regular additions of balanced fertiliser to ensure their health. Citrus trees, however, need a number of trace elements if they are to grow well. Containerised plants are completely reliant upon you for their nutrition. Rain and tap water contain very few nutrients, so the only chemicals available to the tree are those that were in the original compost or those subsequently added by you. Every time you water the container, the existing nutrients in the soil are leached out. Plants with poor nutrition will have stunted growth and yellow leaves and may produce few, if any, fruit.

Nutritional deficiencies are unlikely to develop when a correctly balanced fertiliser is used which includes the three major elements and all of the necessary trace chemicals. In the winter citrus trees need a balanced fertiliser that has equal proportions of nitrogen (N), phosphorus (P), and potassium (K), such as a 20–20–20 formula. Higher levels of nitrogen are required in the spring and summer, when an ideal fertiliser would be 25–15–15.

Dry, crystallised fertiliser works out considerably cheaper than the ready-to-use diluted alternative. Several commercial products are available. The Dorset-based company Global Orange Groves was the first to supply a specialised citrus fertiliser in the United Kingdom. It is available as a high-nitrogen product for summer (25–15–15) and as a balanced formula (20–20–20) for winter. Both fertilisers include significant levels of trace elements.

Chempak, a specialist fertiliser company, has now introduced comparable products: a high-nitrogen summer formula (24–14–14) and a balanced winter formula (18–18–18). Both formulas include the trace elements magnesium, boron, copper, iron, manganese, molybdenum, and zinc.

Boron

Boron is highly toxic to many plants, but trace amounts are required for the correct development of leaves. Plants with a boron deficiency suffer from split stems and deformed leaves. Leaf veins split and the foliage falls prematurely from the tree.

Calcium

Calcium is rarely added to citrus fertiliser because there is usually plenty in the soil or tap water. However, a calcium deficiency can develop if you plant a containerised citrus tree in ericaceous compost and irrigate it with rainwater. Plants with a calcium deficiency have chlorotic leaves, stunted growth and, in severe cases, rotting roots. Calcium deficiency rarely occurs when plants are grown in normal soil.

Copper

While copper is an important element for plant growth, it is also highly toxic if used in excessive quantities. Growers in Florida used to have a problem with a physiological condition called dieback, until it was discovered that it could be cured by the addition of small quantities of copper to fertilisers. Copper can be deficient in peat-based composts (Oliver 1993).

Iron

Iron deficiency is a common problem on calcareous soils and may also occur with containerised plants. Excessive levels of lime can build up when plants are regularly watered with hard water. Lime prevents the iron in the soil from being absorbed by the tree's roots and results in a very distinct form of chlorosis, with the bright green veins of the leaf standing out against a pale yellow background. Older leaves are less affected than younger ones, which become almost entirely yellow and smaller as the deficiency becomes more serious. Containerised plants can be cured by the addition of flowers of sulphur to the soil. This supplement reduces the pH

▶ Chlorosis is usually caused by a mineral deficiency, but can also occur if there is too much lime in the soil. These leaves also show red spider mite damage.

and allows the iron and other minerals to become available to the plant.

Magnesium

The metal magnesium is an essential component of chlorophyll, an organic compound that is necessary for photosynthesis. The first sign of a magnesium deficiency is chlorosis of the leaves, with yellow areas developing in the leaf between the veins and on either side of the midrib. If the deficiency continues, the yellow areas coalesce and the whole leaf eventually becomes yellow. The main consequence of yellow leaves is that the citrus tree cannot photosynthesise correctly and becomes progressively weaker. A magnesium deficiency can be corrected with a foliar feed or by adding a balanced citrus fertiliser to the soil.

Manganese

Manganese deficiency results in a form of chlorosis, with yellowing of the areas between the veins. This problem can be corrected by adding a fertiliser with the correct trace elements.

Molybdenum

The absence of molybdenum causes a physiological disorder called yellow spot. Small pale green or yellow spots appear on the leaves. Affected plants should be watered with a citrus fertiliser.

Nitrogen

Nitrogen is probably the most important component of any fertiliser. It is found in chlorophyll, amino acids, and proteins and is essential for healthy plant growth. Deficient trees have yellow leaves and weak growth and produce a poor crop of fruit. Citrus trees should be given plenty of nitrogen in the spring and summer, but a more balanced fertiliser in the autumn. Excessive nitrogen in the autumn will result in soft growth, which is easily damaged by frost and inclement weather.

Phosphorus

Phosphorus is an important component of DNA and essential for life. The mature leaves of deficient plants develop large brown spots and eventually drop off.

Potassium

Potassium is essential for plant growth and fruit development. The leaves of phosphate-deficient plants develop irregular lesions.

Sulphur

The element sulphur is also necessary for plant growth. Orange fruit are smaller than usual in sulphur-deficient plants, are misshapen, and fail to develop their normal orange colour. The deficiency is most obvious in young growth, which is stunted and yellow. The problem can be corrected by the addition of flowers of sulphur.

Zinc

Citrus trees with a zinc deficiency suffer from a condition called mottle-leaf or frenching. Large patches of yellow tissue appear between the main veins, which remain green. Younger leaves are more seriously affected than older ones, while growth and fruit yields suffer. The deficiency can be cured by the addition of zinc sulphate.

Damaging Compounds in Soil

Lime

Tap water generally has some calcium carbonate dissolved in it. Most tap water is obtained from subterranean aquifers, which have taken hundreds of years to develop. Rainwater is slightly acid when it reaches the ground, having absorbed positively charged hydrogen ions from the atmosphere as it falls. As the rain leaches through the ground, it dissolves calcium carbonate from the ground rock. The amount of calcium carbonate or lime in the water depends upon the area where you live. Hard water contains a lot of lime, while soft contains relatively little.

The amount of calcium dissolved in tap water is not a problem in itself, but as the citrus tree transpires, it leaves the lime behind in the soil. Eventually the level of lime in the soil becomes so high that it prevents the plant roots from absorbing enough nutrients. Citrus trees seem to do best when the soil is slightly acid, but over time the pH is likely to rise so that it becomes alkaline.

The pH of the soil and the level of lime can be controlled by adding a pale yellow powder called flowers of sulphur. The sulphur reacts with the calcium to form calcium sulphate, better known as gypsum, and the pH of the soil subsequently falls. While this type of 'bucket chemistry' is quite effective, chemical salts will still accumulate over time and it is a good idea to replace the top few centimetres (or inches) of compost when you re-pot a citrus tree.

Salt

Common salt, sodium chloride, is a constituent of desert soil and limits where citrus trees can be grown commercially. Citrus trees are very sensitive to salt and can be killed by relatively low concentrations. Salt is normally leached out of the soil by rain, but where land is artificially irrigated, the level of salt can rise significantly.

In lemons excessive levels of salt cause the leaves to turn yellow, curl, and burn at the edges. Eventually the leaves drop off the tree. A few months later the tree produces a new flush of healthy-looking foliage, which then suffers the same fate. Oranges suffer in a slightly different way. The older, more mature foliage turns slightly brown and curls. Finally, all of the leaves fall off the tree. Most citrus trees will recover from salt damage as long as they are irrigated with plenty of fresh, salt-free water.

▲ California State Citrus Park near Riverside has a large collection of citrus trees and is open to the public.

6 Growing Citrus Trees

Successful cultivation of citrus begins at the nursery or garden centre with the selection of a healthy, vibrant plant and is followed by careful attention to the plant's temperature, moisture, and light requirements. In warmer climates, these needs can be adequately met in the open garden, but in temperate climates, the home gardener will want to consider indoor accommodation—at least in cooler weather. Other cultural issues for the home gardener include pruning, grafting, and eventually storing the fruit.

Choosing a Plant

Citrus trees can live for many years if they are carefully looked after, and it therefore makes sense to buy a good quality tree. Furthermore, they are quite expensive to purchase, so it is important to choose your plants carefully. Most garden centres or nurseries will have a number of specimens of each cultivar available. Wherever possible, try to select a plant that has a single upright stem, between 45 and 50 centimetres (18–20 in.) high, rather than a multistemmed bush that branches close to the ground. Plants that branch close to the ground look quite attractive when they are young, but can be difficult to prune when they are older. Standard trees, with a long straight stem, tend to be more expensive but make more attractive specimens in the long term.

When choosing a plant, look for one that has plenty of glossy leaves and inspect it carefully for pests, such as scale insects and mealy bugs. Scale insects are almost impossible to eradicate once they are present and you will be doing yourself a favour by walking away and buying your plant elsewhere if the plant has these pests. If the weather is cold outside, it is a good idea to have the plant put in a polythene bag before you take it to the car. When you get home, place the tree in a bright position away from a central heating radiator and any cold drafts.

Many citrus plants look very similar and the cultivars can only be distinguished when mature fruit are present. Young trees are usually identified by a printed plastic label tied around the stem. The label may be very informative, providing the name of the cultivar and the rootstock onto which it has been grafted. Citrus are becoming more popular in northern Europe, and a lot of garden centres are offering a selection of trees for sale. Many of these trees have originated from hotter countries such as Italy and Spain, where the growing conditions are very different from those in northern Europe. A rootstock that is suitable for the Mediterranean may not be suitable for a colder climate. The rootstock is very important because it has a great effect upon how the grafted scion will grow. There are several rootstocks available, but you won't go far wrong if you choose a tree that has been grafted onto the rootstock of a trifoliate orange (*Poncirus trifoliata*) or one of its cultivars (for example, 'Flying Dragon').

Many plants are offered with a coloured label and simply called an orange tree or lemon. These are likely to be a well-known cultivar such as Seville orange or 'Eureka' lemon, but there is no guarantee. My advice is to buy a named cultivar rather than something of unknown origin.

It is a fact of life that labels get mixed up and young trees are often incorrectly labelled. This doesn't matter so much with an herbaceous perennial, but a citrus tree costs considerably more and, if treated correctly, will live for several decades. It is worth asking a nursery about its policy on replacing mislabelled trees. I have purchased trees from reputable nurseries only to find several years later that the tree wasn't what I expected. It is very difficult to argue for the replacement of a tree when you have had it for ten years. Whatever you do, it is wise to keep the receipt in case you need to return the plant.

Many commercial citrus trees are far too big to be grown in a greenhouse and have to be grafted onto a dwarfing rootstock to keep them to a sensible size. Grapefruit, for example, may grow to a height of 10 metres (33 ft.) outdoors and, given the correct conditions, will attempt to do the same in a heated greenhouse!

Most plants available to the home gardener will, in all likelihood, have been grafted onto a semi-dwarfing rootstock, such as trifoliate orange, which will reduce the size of a mature tree by approximately 50 percent. The range of plants that are available and the rootstock that they have been grafted onto will depend to a great extent upon where you live. Most of the plants that are available for sale in British nurseries and garden centres will have been field grown in Spain or Italy and grafted onto 'Troyer' or 'Carrizo' citrange or trifoliate orange rootstocks.

A number of these nurseries also supply trees that are certified as being virus-free. This is less important in a cold climate than in a warmer one where citrus trees are grown as a commercial crop, but a virus-free plant will always grow better than one that is infected with a virus. 'Meyer' lemon has always been a popular plant in colder countries because it needs lower temperatures than a true lemon and can be propagated by taking cuttings. However, the original 'Meyer' lemon is a symptomless carrier for citrus tristeza disease and could transfer this disease to the other plants in your collection. It is quite possible that some of the less-specialised nurseries in northern Europe are still selling the original 'Meyer' lemon and completely unaware that it is a carrier for a serious viral disease. Always ensure that you are buying an 'Improved Meyer' lemon.

Several of the plants available from northern nurseries are no longer grown commercially and have been superseded by improved cultivars in other countries. Some such as the 'Improved Meyer' have proved unsuitable for commercial use, but make excellent backyard plants. Many cultivars of lemon are only used locally and have little economic significance, while others are grown around the world and have been given local names.

Growing Citrus in a Temperate Climate

Most people who live in a temperate climate consider that citrus trees are rather exotic plants and would never attempt to grow them in their own garden. However, citrus trees are very ornamental and make wonderful pot plants. In the spring they are covered with extremely fragrant blossoms and, if you can overwinter them at the correct temperature, you may be able to enjoy fresh fruit throughout the year. Children love orange trees and are fascinated when you are able to produce your own juice, without buying it from the supermarket in a cardboard carton. Citrus are also far tougher than people realise and, as far as I can recollect, I have never lost a citrus tree through cold damage. Mice have eaten them, one plant died from overwatering, and another was stolen, but none have died from frost damage. I'm sure my neighbours think that I am rather eccentric, but by one means or another I have managed to keep the great majority of my trees alive for twenty years.

Most people would laugh if you suggested that it would be a good idea to plant an orange orchard in England. However, this is precisely what Sir Francis Carew did during the middle of the sixteenth century, possibly because there were no books around to tell him that it wouldn't work! His trees (presumably sour orange) were planted in the open ground and a large wooden structure was erected around them during the winter to protect the plants from the English weather. The roof supports were permanent, but the remainder of the structure was presumably kept in store during the summer and then re-erected in the autumn. Now I am not suggesting that everyone should go out and plant an orange orchard in their back garden, but it would be interesting to try.

Some *Citrus* species will tolerate surprisingly low levels of sunlight when they are dormant during the winter. However, they are not suitable for growing as houseplants and need plenty of sunshine during the summer when they are actively growing. They should be kept reasonably dry during the winter months, but will still need regular watering if the weather is mild. It is important to realise that citrus trees transpire a lot of water, even when they are partially dormant, and it has to go somewhere. The moisture may not be apparent, but it will condense on cold surfaces and may cause problems with mould or even result in dry rot (*Serpula lacrymans*). Dry rot is a pernicious disease because it may not be apparent until it is too late. The mycelia can travel over, and sometimes through, non-woody structural components, such as bricks and girders, until they find a suitable timber. Wood is only vulnerable if the internal moisture level rises above 20 percent. Good ventilation is therefore essential and will also prevent the plants from overheating on a sunny day.

Temperate gardeners may also be tempted to grow some of the more unusual varieties of sour orange and lemon. These were quite popular in the past and were illustrated in Ferrari's *Hesperides* (1646), Volkamer's *Nürbergische Hesperides* (1708–1714), and Risso and Poiteau's *Histoire naturelle des orangers* (1818–1822). Some of these plants have survived in old citrus collections, such as the very strange form of sour orange called 'Bizzaria', which is probably a chimera with a citron, and 'Adam's Apple', which is probably a cross between a citron, a pummelo, and a lemon. As interest in citrus grows, these plants are likely to be re-introduced into nurseries and will become more readily available to the interested gardener.

Temperature

Among citrus, limes are the most sensitive to frost, followed by grapefruit, sweet and sour oranges, lemons, clementines, and finally satsumas, which can tolerate remarkably low temperatures. The minimum winter temperature for most citrus is 10°C (50°F), but many will survive much lower temperatures for a short period of time, as long as they do not actually freeze. Very cold temperatures will damage the tree's wood, kill its fruit, and cause severe defoliation. Some citrus fruit can take up to eighteen months to mature and this can be difficult to achieve unless you have a warm place to keep the citrus trees during the cold winter months.

It therefore makes sense to select plants that you will able to grow, rather than something that will struggle for several years and eventually give up the ghost. Pummelos are a good example; they need very high temperatures to produce edible fruit and form very large trees that are too big for the average conservatory.

Most of the information concerning the hardiness of citrus in a cold climate is anecdotal and very little has been published about the subject. Most of our knowledge is based upon the performance of citrus trees in commercial orchards, in much warmer climates.

One of the most interesting objective studies of cold hardiness was published by Rieger et al. in 2003. The team assembled a collection of sixteen cultivars and close relatives of the genus *Citrus* that were believed to have good cold tolerance. The plants were grown under controlled conditions in the Coastal Gardens Research Farm, approximately 32 kilometres (20 m) inland from the coast of Savannah, Georgia, in the United States. The plants included 'Meiwa' and 'Nagami' kumquats, 'Meyer' lemon, 'Eustis' limequat, 'Changsha' mandarin, 'Owari' Satsuma, and *Citrus ichangensis*.

The results were very surprising considering that all of these plants are recognised as having a good degree of cold hardiness. The 'Meyer' lemon, 'Eustis' limequat, and all three kumquats died or suffered from 100 percent dieback during the first winter. Only four plants were considered to be completely cold hardy at the end of the experiment: 'Owari' Satsuma, 'Changsha' mandarin, 'Mr. John's Longevity' citrangequat, and 'Nippon' orangequat.

'Owari' Satsuma is known to be hardy, but it suffered no dieback and only 50 percent defoliation at the end of the first winter. It also survived four nights with temperatures down to −6°C (22°F) during the winter of 1998–99 and thirteen nights where the temperature fell to −8°C (18°F) in

The incredibly hardy 'Owari' Satsuma forms an attractive, weeping bush.

'Owari' Satsuma should be the first choice for anyone trying to grow citrus fruit in a cold climate.

2001–02. The razzlequat (which the study authors believed was a hybrid between the dessert plant *Eremocitrus glauca* and an unknown kumquat, but was probably a eremolemon) was considered to be the hardiest of all, but had the disadvantage of being very thorny. (There does not appear to be any such thing as a razzlequat. The suffix *-quat* would be the correct term for a hybrid with a kumquat, but the prefix *razzle-* appears to have been invented.)

This surprising result suggests that 'Owari' Satsuma should be the first choice for anyone trying to grow citrus trees in a cold climate. My own plant has always shown incredible hardiness and produces a small crop of edible fruit, without fail, every year. It is less vigorous than some of my other plants, but puts on a modest amount of growth every year.

Watering and Overwatering

Careful watering is extremely important with citrus. Plants may need to be watered every day during hot weather, but only require watering once a week or even less frequently in the winter. They should always be watered so that the soil is saturated with water.

When watering citrus, it is extremely important to give them a really good soaking, so that air is drawn through the plant and nutrients are distributed throughout the compost. A medium-sized citrus tree in a dry 30-centimetre (15-in.) pot will absorb approximately 4 litres (1 U.S. gallon) of water during the summer. The compost should be watered until the liquid starts to run out from the bottom of the pot. This ensures that potentially damaging salts are flushed out of the compost and air is drawn down through the root system. To be certain that the compost is saturated, it is a good idea to add further water and allow it to drain out as well. Do not water the plant again until the compost has started to dry out and do not allow it to stand in water.

Whenever possible, citrus trees should be watered with clean rainwater. Tap water may be more convenient but in many areas it is treated with small levels of chlorine to control water-borne pathogens and fluoride to reduce tooth decay in the human population. Chlorine concentrations as low as 200 ppm have been shown to cause slight damage to lemon trees, and the dissolved lime in tap water leaves unsightly marks on the foliage if it is sprayed during the summer. Tap water is less of a problem with outdoor plants because the toxic chemicals are leached out of the soil by rainfall.

Plants in small pots are more likely to become water-stressed than those in large ones. Containerised citrus can be drip-fed, but it is a difficult balance. Containerised citrus trees may also need to be watered during wet weather as mature trees usually develop a dense canopy of foliage, which prevents natural rainfall from reaching the pot. It might be pouring with rain outside, but the compost is still dry.

Citrus are quite tolerant plants, but if you forget to water them during the summer they are likely to die. Young leaves will become distorted if you stop watering for too long and any flower buds will fall off the tree. If you are going away on holiday in the summer, it is essential to find someone who is willing to water your plants, which may need watering on a daily basis during the hottest days of the summer. While drip hoses can help, they can become blocked or the timer may cease to work correctly.

Citrus should never be allowed to stand in water; this will lead to root rot and the possible demise of the plant. Another common error is to give plants a little water every day. This creates a patch of permanently wet soil at the top of the pot, while the remainder is bone dry. On sunny days it is quite common for the surface of the compost to dry out, even though the remainder is quite moist. When this happens it is tempting to give it some more water, but more plants die from overwatering than drought.

Overwatering is less of a problem when citrus trees are planted in loam-based compost and a terracotta pot, but this will add significantly to their weight. Most citrus trees are field-grown and are transferred into a peat-based compost before they are sold to the customer. Peat-based composts are very light, but they often retain too much water and excessive watering will usually result in the death of the citrus tree. Overwatered trees look rather sickly; their foliage turns yellow and then falls off unless the amount of watering is quickly reduced.

If a plant loses all of its leaves and you suspect that it has been overwatered, carefully turn it upside down and remove it from the pot. Healthy roots will be strong and white in the centre, while dead ones will be dark brown, have no cortex, and easily break if they are pulled. (These same symptoms can also be caused by fibrous root rot, *Phytophthora*, so if the plant doesn't recover, throw it away and dispose of the compost and pot.) The plant may be beyond recovery, but it is worth trying to rescue it. Remove the excess compost and cut the roots back until you reach healthy ones. The tree should be re-potted in fresh compost and the aerial branches cut back to a healthy looking bud (the damaged root system will not be able to support as much foliage as before). Watering should be kept to a minimum until new shoots appear. If all of the roots have rotted, the plant will have to be thrown away.

Overwintering Citrus

In an ideal world all gardeners in temperate climates would have a large, heated greenhouse or a conservatory, where they could admire their carefully nurtured plants. In reality, a large conservatory is beyond the financial means of many people, but this shouldn't stop them from growing citrus plants. Gardeners in hotter countries would be amazed at the lengths to which people in cooler ones go to grow citrus trees. Temporary structures can be made from timber and polythene, which, while not ideal, are often sufficient to keep the plants alive during the cold winter months.

Elsewhere in this chapter I talk about greenhouses and conservatories, but let me clarify one thing from the beginning—citrus trees are not houseplants. Most houses are too dark and, if centrally heated, have air that is too dry for citrus plants. Citrus trees can be taken indoors during the winter if there is no alternative, but they must be kept cool. Central heating provides a comfortable living environment for humans, but from a plant's perspective being in such an environment is equivalent to living in the Sahara Desert.

Citrus are remarkably tolerant plants, but they resent sudden changes in their environment and often respond by shedding their foliage. Leaf drop is quite distressing for the plant's owner, particularly if he or she has just paid a lot of money for a relatively mature tree. Depending upon the cause, citrus trees will usually produce a fresh crop of leaves in the spring, so the incident is rarely fatal. However, leaf drop does weaken the plant and can make it more susceptible to attack by pests and diseases. The best way to avoid leaf drop is to keep the thermostat for your central heating turned down to a fairly low temperature when the plants are first brought indoors and spray them with lukewarm water to maintain the humidity. The plants will quickly acclimatise to their new circumstances and the temperature can be gradually increased to a more comfortable level, but should never rise above about 15°C (59°F). The plants still need plenty of light in the winter and the compost should be kept reasonably dry.

There is no need to panic if your citrus trees lose their leaves, but it is important to identify the cause. If your trees have lost their foliage because you forgot to water them, do not overcompensate by watering them every subsequent day. The plant cannot transpire as much water as before because it has lost its foliage and you will only compound the problem by making the compost waterlogged. Plants that have suffered from leaf drop can be pruned during the following spring, by reducing the new shoots to one-third of their original length. This will stimulate the production of more buds and eventually create a more luxuriant bush. The tree can be left as it is, but you are likely to end up with several bare branches, with tufts of young leaves at the tips.

Leaf drop is likely to occur during the autumn when citrus trees are adapting to the lower humidity levels of a greenhouse or conservatory. To reduce leaf drop caused by sudden changes to the plant's environment, you can prepare a plant for its winter home. Towards the end of summer place your citrus trees in a shady position in the garden, so that they can acclimatise to lower levels of sunshine, and reduce the amount of watering. If you are fortunate enough to own a conservatory, you can immediately move the plants into it, but if no conservatory is available, the plants can be overwintered in your home as long you place them in a bright position and turn the heating off in that room.

Moving Plants Outdoors

We all look forward to the spring, but it has dangers for the unwary gardener in temperate climates where a late frost can easily damage a citrus placed outdoors after having been overwintered successfully. The British Isles, for example, have quite a mild climate, but frosts may still occur in May and even early June. It is therefore important to prepare citrus for their 'spring migration' from late April onwards.

It is a good idea not to water the plants immediately before you move them, because this will significantly increase the weight of the pot. For the first few weeks outdoors in spring, the trees should be placed in a sheltered position where they do not receive the full strength of the sun. After a couple of weeks the plants can be moved into a sunnier position and watered normally.

Mature trees may need watering every day in very hot weather, but should only be fed once a week. Citrus will always grow more luxuriantly if they are sprayed with soft water on sunny days. If you live in an area with hard water, it is a good idea to use rainwater.

Conditions outdoors are very different and plants need to be well watered if they are to cope with the greatly increased levels of sunlight. Blustery winds can also damage foliage, and citrus trees are best kept in a sheltered spot until the young leaves have matured. Containerised plants grow very quickly when they are taken outside and will usually produce new buds within three to four weeks. Young foliage and developing fruit are particularly susceptible to sun scorch and should be protected from excessive sunlight.

Some gardeners go to incredible lengths to maintain their citrus plants. My own neighbours said that they didn't need a weather forecast; they knew when a frost was due because the citrus plants would suddenly disappear off my front drive.

Most citrus need a minimum temperature of 10°C (50°F) if they are to grow well, but, with the exception of limes, most will survive as long as the temperature does not fall below 4°C (39°F). Frost will cause serious damage to most citrus, which should be moved indoors if this appears likely.

As temperatures fall during the autumn the trees become semidormant and are more capable of withstanding cold. Fruit may be damaged during cold weather and leaves will lose their shine, but the trees should survive until the following spring, as long as they do not freeze. Very little water is required during this period and plants in soil-based compost appear to fare better in cold weather than those in an organic, peat-based medium.

Weather Damage

Citrus trees can be damaged in stormy weather and should be placed in a sheltered position where they are protected from the prevailing wind. The trees often produce new buds throughout the spring and summer and these can be damaged by gusts of wind. It is also a good idea to check the plants from time to time to ensure that there is no damage to the crown of the tree. A heavy crop of fruit may cause the branch to split away from the main stem, effectively splitting the tree in two. This tends to be more of a problem with containerised trees because they are not as vigorous as those growing outside throughout the year and growth may be intermittent. If a branch splits away from the main stem it should be removed with a saw. The rest of the tree may look unbalanced, but it is better to leave heavy pruning until the spring when the new season's growth start. The tree should recover as long as the scion hasn't been too badly damaged and there is at least one remaining bud on the stem. If the worst has happened and the scion is damaged beyond repair it may be possible to graft a new piece of budwood onto the rootstock.

Growing Citrus in a Greenhouse or Conservatory

Most people in cooler countries have to rely upon conservatories and greenhouses to grow tender garden plants.

Greenhouses

A large greenhouse is a valuable asset for any gardener and comes into its own if the gardener has a large collection of citrus trees. Greenhouses can be used for growing citrus year-round as long as they have plenty of ventilation and are shaded during the summer months. However, the majority of domestic greenhouses do not have sufficient ventilation and most people cannot be bothered to erect shading or to paint the glass with a reflective coating.

Most citrus will tolerate high temperatures if they have enough water, but the fruit are likely to cook on the tree or be shed over the following days. Containerised citrus are more vulnerable than citrus that are planted out in a greenhouse border. The latter can be watered with a drip irrigator, but it is important to ensure that the ground never becomes waterlogged and is allowed to dry between watering events. The irrigation should be controlled by an electronic timer and is best carried out in the evening or early morning. Aerial misting will keep the plants healthy and ensure that they have glossy dark green foliage. It is best to use rainwater for aerial misting because hard tap water will leave unattractive lime-scale deposits on the leaves.

Greenhouses are useful for overwintering containerised citrus, but if you intend to keep the plants permanently under glass the trees are better planted in open borders, where the roots can develop naturally and regular watering is less important. The trees will grow very quickly in these circumstances and will need to be pruned on a regular basis to prevent them from growing too large.

Unfortunately, open borders also provide a wonderful opportunity for weeds and these can harbour pests and diseases. Chemical weed killers only provide a temporary solution to this problem and there is a risk that the spray will drift onto the trees and cause serious damage. A better alternative for suppressing weeds is to use groundcover perennials or UV-inhibited black woven polypropylene fabric. The latter is widely used in the nursery trade and has the advantage that it will not harbour pests. The material is permeable to water and can be camouflaged with gravel to make it appear more attractive.

Conservatories

Conservatories have become extremely popular in Europe since the 1980s and they provide a perfect winter home for citrus. Most are double glazed and centrally heated, which enables the owner to maintain the interior at room temperature (20°C, or 68°F) without incurring exorbitant fuel bills. A well-designed conservatory is the ideal place to overwinter citrus trees, but it must be well ventilated and should have a tiled floor. Roof vents provide the best type of ventilation, because they allow hot air to rise and escape out of the top of the building. Automatic vents will operate when you are out of the house, but can present a potential trap for wild birds.

Many conservatories are carpeted, but it is very difficult to keep the carpet in good condition if the building is full of plants. Containerised citrus should be placed in plastic saucers to reduce the risk of spillage, but it is quite easy to overwater a citrus plant, particularly if it is growing in a soil-based compost. Excess water eventually drains out of the pot and fills up the saucer, with any surplus draining onto the floor. While this can be wiped up, a small amount often seeps under the pot and causes a wet patch. Such leakage is not a problem with a tiled surface, but carpets will turn mouldy if they are kept permanently damp. The worst of the mould can usually be removed if the problem is discovered at an early stage, but in the longer term the carpet will become stained as the mould digests the carpet fibres. Condensation can also be a problem and patches of water may develop under the saucer without you realising it.

Conservatories should be provided with plenty of shading if the citrus trees are going to be kept in the building during the summer. The location of the shading will depend upon the orientation of the conservatory, but south- or west-facing structures tend to become extremely hot in the summer. Excess heat will damage the trees and may result in them dropping their leaves. Curtains are very useful and will help to keep the conservatory warm in the winter. Central heating is more acceptable in a conservatory than in a house, because so much of the heat escapes through the glass. While central heating will keep the room warm in the winter, it also makes the air very dry, which is detrimental to good plant health. The plants will greatly benefit from being sprayed regularly with de-ionised water or rainwater, which should be kept at room temperature. Most citrus trees will produce a good crop of fruit if they are overwintered in a conservatory. Large plants should be placed on four-wheeled dollies, so that they can be pushed out of the way when you are entertaining or need to clean the conservatory.

The high light levels in conservatories during the summer make them ideal for growing citrus, and the lower light levels during the winter allow the plants to have a dormant phase, albeit less pronounced than if they were outside and thus a small amount of growth continues to take place. The compost will need watering less frequently in the winter than in the summer, but it should not be allowed to dry out completely. Feeding should be continued in winter, but using a balanced fertiliser with lower levels of nitrogen (for example, 20–20–20). The plants will benefit from occasional misting with lukewarm rainwater; this removes dust from the leaves and helps to maintain a more humid atmosphere. Citrus need a period of dormancy during the winter and the temperature should, if possible, be reduced to between 10 and 15°C (50–59°F) from October to March. This cold period allows the previous year's wood to harden.

Most builders will construct a conservatory so that the internal ground level is above the surrounding land, or the threshold of the door frame is raised to prevent rain or floodwater from entering the building. However, mature citrus trees can become extreme heavy, and if they are planted in a soil-based compost, it may be almost impossible to move them from the conservatory into the garden and vice versa. Most eighteenth-century orangeries were built so that the floor was flush with the surrounding terrace and plants could be easily moved through the high, purpose-built doorways. This may not seem important in the summer when you are admiring your collection of citrus trees on the patio, but it will become a matter of considerable significance when you are trying to move your potted tree indoors. A small tree planted in a 30-cm (12-in.) terracotta pot that is filled with loam-based compost will weigh about 25 kilograms (55 lbs.). Such heavy pots are best moved using a two-wheeled sack truck or a four-wheeled dolly. Very large citrus trees present more of a problem and are often moved with a forklift truck, in which case the containers are left on a wooden pallet and surrounded by a wooden box during the summer.

Versailles Containers

Versailles containers are almost synonymous with the idea of citrus trees. The design of these elegant wooden containers is usually credited to Jean-Baptiste de La Quintinie (1624–1688), director of the king's kitchen at the Palace of Versailles, in France. The original containers were made from oak, but from Napoleonic times they were constructed with metal posts. While early containers were made in one piece, later models were constructed so that the sides of the box could be removed, making it easier to extract the tree.

True Versailles containers are difficult to find, but worth the investment. Almost all of the commercially available models are made from painted softwood, which rots in a comparatively short period of time. Hardwood containers are preferable, but many people consider the use of teak or mahogany for such purposes unacceptable from an environmental point of view. Several alternatives exist, such as oak, but always ensure that the timber has been sourced from a sustainable, managed forest. There are several

◀ Versailles containers are still the most elegant way of growing citrus trees.

▲ Mature citrus trees may need to be moved with a forklift truck. The pallet and container can be disguised by surrounding it with wooden panels.

schemes for ensuring this, including the internationally recognised Forest Stewardship Council (for more information please visit www.fsc.org/en).

Furniture manufacturers are often wary about admitting where their hardwood timber originates. Salespeople are very adept at avoiding this question, particularly if they have been asked about it previously. Certified products will have the FSC or another recognised printed logo on the label. Unfortunately, some companies will only change their buying policy when they realise that they are losing sales.

Wooden boxes can also be made so that they fit around the containerised tree. The boxes are made in sections and then assembled by using bolts or hooks.

Growing Citrus in a Subtropical or Mediterranean Climate

There is no getting away from the fact that citrus trees are much easier to grow in a hot rather than a cold climate. But, while the trees grow much faster, they are also prone to many pests and diseases.

Commercial citrus trees can be satisfactorily grown outdoors in areas that have a Mediterranean or semi-tropical climate. In the United States this includes most of California, the lower areas of Arizona, and the southern parts of Florida, Louisiana, Mississippi, and Texas.

Citrus trees are fairly tough plants, but they are easily damaged by cold weather and the position that you choose is extremely important. Low-lying sites are best avoided because frost is more likely to form in these situations.

Fans like this one in a citrus orchard in Riverside, California, are used to keep the air circulating on cold nights. The machines are quite effective in stopping ice from forming on trees.

Frost is also most likely to occur on a clear night, when the soil's heat is quickly lost to the sky. The ideal situation is the side of a hill; this should be south-facing in the Northern Hemisphere and north-facing in the Southern. If citrus trees are correctly placed, the cold air will drift past them and accumulate at the bottom of the slope, leaving the trees unaffected. Citrus trees are most vulnerable to frost when they are young and should be protected by wrapping them with fleece or burlap. Fans are often used to disperse the cold and prevent frost from forming on the trees.

Young citrus trees should be chosen with great care and are best obtained from a reliable source. Small plants are the quickest to become established, but larger plants make more of an impact. If possible inspect the plants before you take them home and make sure that no scale insects are present.

It is absolutely essential that the nursery can guarantee its stock is virus-free. Citrus are prone to several serious viral diseases including CTV (citrus tristeza virus), greening, and mal secco. Never buy a plant from a backstreet trader or accept one from a neighbour. It may be cheaper in the short run, but it could prove to be a serious mistake. The plant should be freshly containerised with healthy, dark green foliage and must be free of aphids and scale insects. The latter spread like wildfire in a citrus collection and are almost impossible to eradicate, so it makes sense to prevent them in the first place. If plants are infected with scale insects, you should tell the proprietor and buy your plants elsewhere.

While citrus prefer a well-drained sandy soil, clay soils can be used if you provide plenty of artificial drainage. Drainage can also be improved by incorporating plenty of sand, or by planting the tree on a raised mound of soil. The soil should have a neutral pH. If the soil is acidic, add plenty of ground limestone. Chemical methods of reducing the pH can damage citrus trees, while ground limestone breaks down gradually over time.

Although most young citrus plants are containerised and can be planted at any time of the year, spring is by far the best time to plant them because the risk of frost has passed and the trees have a few weeks to get established before the summer's hot weather. The plants should be thoroughly watered before planting and then removed from their pot. Tease the outer roots away from the compost and place the tree in the prepared hole. Backfill the hole with soil and ensure that the graft union is above ground level. This is important because foot rot (*Phytophthora*) usually infects a plant through the graft union.

Many young plants are supplied with a loose ball of soil, wrapped in a

▶ Citrus trees need regular watering in a hot climate. Majorca.

piece of burlap (known as hessian in the United Kingdom). Place the root ball in the hole and then backfill it with a mixture of soil and compost, again ensuring that the graft union is above ground level. Create a circular basin around the plant that will hold water, but mound the soil up around the trunk so that the water does not come directly into contact with the plant. The basin should not continue beyond the drip line of the tree, that is, beyond the maximum extent of the canopy. The plant should then be watered on a weekly basis until it is well established.

Large collections of trees can be irrigated by drip watering or spraying. Drip watering is the most efficient method because it only applies water where it is needed and consequently reduces the amount of weeding that is necessary. Spraying covers a larger area and is the best way of irrigating large trees, but it can be difficult to control exactly where the water is applied. Whichever method you use, it is important to regularly check that the nozzles are clear. If a nozzle becomes blocked, a tree may remain unwatered for several days and could die.

Irrigation systems use black polythene pipe, which can be buried beneath the ground. The water supply is controlled by a timer, which only applies water in the morning and evening when there is less evaporation. Excessive watering can invite phytophthora and overhead irrigation can spread a number of fungal pathogens, including citrus scab and canker. Nevertheless, it is important to set the timer so that enough water is applied to thoroughly soak the soil down to a depth of 50 centimetres (20 in.) or more.

Young citrus trees require very little pruning when grown outside, other than to retain their shape and removed any dead or damaged branches. Citrus are vulnerable to a number of pests, such as scale insects, mites, whitefly, caterpillars, and grasshoppers.

Cold winds often cause defoliation on the exposed side of the tree. Frost causes browning of the leaves and, if severe, is followed by defoliation. The damage is always greatest on the exposed side of the bush.

Pruning Citrus

Citrus do not require as much pruning as many other fruit trees, and it is not necessary to build up a system of leaders as you would with an apple tree. When citrus plants are established, pruning can be limited to the removal of crossing or damaged branches.

Because citrus produce very heavy fruit, it is important to build up a strong scaffold of branches that are capable of bearing them. In the spring the main branches can be cut back to an outward-facing bud, so that they are approximately 15 to 30 centimetres (6–12 in.) long if grown in containers. Such pruning is not essential, however, and citrus trees can be left to grow naturally with minimal intervention. Short stubs of wood without a bud should not be left on the tree because they often die back and may form a point of weakness. Buds do not always grow where you expect them to; if this happens, prune the remaining stub of wood back to another actively growing bud.

Further pruning is rarely necessary when citrus trees are grown outdoors unless damage occurs. Containerised trees are rarely as vigorous and may sometimes benefit from being pruned in the spring. Unwanted or damaged growth should be pruned back to a healthy bud. If major surgery is required, the cut should be made so that it is flush with the trunk of the tree.

The amount of pruning depends upon the condition of the plant and the location in which it is being grown. Citrus often lose leaves during the winter if they are subjected to a sudden change in temperature and established plants tend to look rather threadbare if their lower leaves have fallen off. Tired looking or damaged citrus trees can be rejuvenated in the spring by cutting back their branches by one-third and allowing them to produce new leaves. The tree will lose any young fruit that may have been developing.

Pathogenic viruses, fungi such as *Phytophthora*, and bacteria can be transferred to other plants as a result of bad hygiene. To avoid this, citrus trees should always be pruned and grafted with sterilised or disinfected implements.

Suckers and Water Shoots

Citrus trees sometime produce several vertical shoots with an acute angle between them. These are very vulnerable to damage when the tree is older and the problem should be rectified as soon as possible. A heavy load of

◀ Mature citrus trees can be heavily pruned to keep them in shape in a container.

▶ Rootstocks often produce suckers. These leggy growths should be removed as soon as possible before they weaken the grafted tree.

fruit may cause the stem to split vertically and cause permanent, irretrievable damage. The best way to resolve this is to remove the upper growth as soon as it has happened and prune it back to a lower bud. The cut stem should grow normally and allow a stronger branch to develop.

Trifoliate orange rootstocks often produce suckers, which may occur at any point below the graft union but are usually found at ground level. Suckers should be removed as soon as possible to prevent them from growing at the expense of the scion.

Citrus trees occasionally produce water shoots, which are very vigorous and flattened in section. Water shoots grow very quickly and will upset the balance of the tree unless they are controlled. They can be either removed completely or pruned back to restore the balance of the tree. Pruned water shoots usually grow normally in subsequent years.

Growing Citrus from Pips

Children love growing plants from seeds, and citrus can be particularly rewarding. Citrus trees often exhibit parthenogenesis and the seeds consequently have the same genetic make-up as their parent. Although the seeds generally grow into perfectly acceptable citrus plants, most seedlings are likely to succumb to damping-off disease. Very few are likely to survive long enough to produce any fruit because they are also vulnerable to root rot (*Phytophthora*). Your chances of success will be greatly increased by grafting them onto a rootstock.

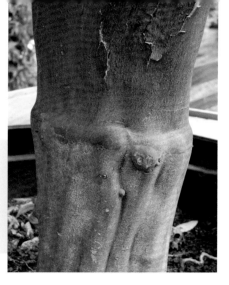

▶ The graft can leave a large scar on some citrus trees.

▲ The union between a rootstock and a scion is often apparent in older trees.

Commercial growers can choose from a number of suitable rootstocks, but amateurs are best advised to stick to trifoliate orange (*Poncirus trifoliata*), which is also easily grown from seed and has good cold tolerance. It is very compatible with sweet oranges, but less so with mandarins and is inclined to produce smaller fruit when used as a rootstock for grapefruit. Citrus trees that have been grafted onto a trifoliate orange rootstock require soil with a pH of between 5.5 and 6.5.

Grafting Citrus

Grafting has a long history and was used by the ancient Greeks and Chinese. Propagation is best carried out during the main growing period when the trees are at their most vigorous, normally between May and August. Only virus-free material should be propagated.

Several rootstocks are available for grafting, but trifoliate orange (*Poncirus trifoliata*) is probably the best choice in a relatively cold climate. This rootstock tolerates cold and wet soil and is ideal for plants that are going to be containerised. The citranges 'Troyer' and 'Carrizo' also have good cold tolerance.

Young rootstocks are obtained by sowing seeds from selected fruit. The seeds are easily damaged and should be sown immediately in sterilised seed compost. Germination takes approximately three weeks at 13°C (55°F) and the young seedlings are kept until they are between eighteen months and two years old. By this stage their stems will be approximately 10–15 millimetres (3/8–5/8 in.) in diameter.

It is very important to use a sharp grafting knife and to disinfect it with a 10-percent solution of sodium hypochlorite (domestic bleach). Citrus trees are usually grafted by making an inverted T-shaped cut in the side of the rootstock. To prevent soil-borne pathogens from infecting the scion, the graft union should be made between 20 and 30 centimetres (8–12 in.) above the ground. The first cut is made down the length of the stem and the second at right angles to it. Buds are removed from the donating tree by making a cut approximately 1 centimetre (3/8 in.) beneath it and ending approximately 1 centimetre above it. The bark of the rootstock is carefully prised apart where the two cuts intersect and the budwood pushed firmly into it.

The completed graft is wrapped with grafting tape, ensuring that the inserted budwood is still visible. The grafting tape applies sufficient pressure to keep the budwood in contact with the rootstock and prevents dirt and water from entering the cut. The graft should be inspected after approximately one month. The bud in a successful union will remain green while a dead one will turn black.

Grafted plants are brought into growth by placing them in a warm greenhouse. After a month or so the main shoot above the graft is removed with a sharp, sterile knife. The loss of the apical shoot will stimulate the grafted bud and those of the rootstock to grow. All of the shoots from the rootstock should be rubbed out to allow the grafted scion to grow successfully. The young plants should be protected from windy weather because the young growth is very vulnerable to damage. If the scion fails to take, the rootstock can be reused.

Fruit Production

Citrus are highly productive. Even small, recently grafted trees will produce a number of fruit. It is very tempting to allow your new acquisition to produce fruit, but it places a considerable stress on the tree. Some citrus, and particularly limes, are so fecund that they will still produce fruit when most of the foliage has fallen off the tree.

Young plants should only be allowed to produce fruit in the second and preferably the third year after grafting. The quality of the fruit will depend upon the age of the tree, the rootstock, watering regime, how well the tree has been cared for, and finally, and most importantly, how warm it was during the winter months. Most citrus flower during the spring and their fruit are harvested in the following winter or early spring. Others, such as

grapefruit, may take more than a year to mature and require temperatures that are almost impossible to maintain in a cool climate.

Most commercial citrus growers aim to produce fruit with as few seeds as possible and plant their trees in large blocks of a single cultivar. This is impossible for the home gardener who will usually have a single specimen of each, so you have to accept that your fruit are likely to have plenty of seeds.

Keeping Citrus Fruit

Most harvested citrus fruit will start to deteriorate after a few days when stored at room temperature. The first sign of damage is shrinking skin, followed by a loss of firmness, and then a deterioration of flavour. Eventually the fruit will start to shrivel and may be infected by moulds, which will cause it to rot. Rotting is more likely to occur if the fruit are in contact with one another. The fruit will last longer if they are kept in the main compartment of your refrigerator, but may start to develop brown spots after a few weeks. Oranges can be stored at lower temperatures than grapefruit, which are best kept between 7 and 9°C (45 to 48°F). Some people recommend keeping citrus fruit in individual plastic bags, but this may promote the development of fungi.

The best way to store citrus is to leave them on the tree. Some cultivars last longer than others. 'Valencia' orange, in particular, can be left on the tree for several months without showing much sign of deterioration. Others, such as 'Thomson' navel orange, have to be harvested as soon as they have ripened or they start to deteriorate within a few weeks. This is one of the main advantages of growing your own citrus trees. Many recipes only need a single citrus fruit and these are readily available if you have your own collection.

▲ Recently pollinated citrus trees produce plenty of young fruit, but the majority will fall off after a few weeks. This natural process prevents the tree from carrying too much fruit and is not the result of bad cultivation.

7 Pests and Diseases

I think that it is fair to say that citrus trees suffer from more than their fair share of pests and diseases. Most of these are only a problem in warmer countries, but they have serious economic consequences. Many countries have imposed strict rules on the import of citrus fruit and budwood, because of the pathogens or pests that they can harbour. In the United States, citrus plants cannot be shipped from one growing area to another and a complete quarantine has been imposed upon Florida, where citrus canker must now be considered out of control.

Tourists are sometimes tempted to take a cutting when they see a new and interesting plant while on vacation. You should never do this with citrus plants because you may inadvertently introduce a new virus, pest, or disease to your home country. The implications of this do not bear thinking about. The citrus industry is worth a lot of money and appears to be fighting a losing battle in the war against pests and diseases. If you see an interesting citrus plant when you are away, leave it where it is. It is highly likely that a local nursery will be able to supply you with a plant in any case.

Viruses and Bacteria

Viruses are responsible for a number of serious citrus diseases, so wherever possible it is best to buy certified, virus-free stock. The virus can be removed under laboratory conditions by cutting off the apical meristem from the extreme tip of the shoot. This selects the young cells before the virus is able to infect them. Virus-free material has to be grown in a special greenhouse where potential vectors, such as aphids, are excluded.

Penicillium Mould

Two species of *Penicillium* cause damage to citrus fruit: green mould

(*P. glaucum*) and blue mould (*P. italicum*). Fungal damage is most likely to occur in dry rather than wet conditions. Blue mould can be spread by contact. The fungi often appear on stored fruit.

Sooty Mould

Sooty moulds are common saprophytic fungi that live on the honeydew exuded by sap-sucking insects. Most are common in the soil and on rotting plant material and include species from the genera *Aureobasidium*, *Antennariella*, *Capnodium*, *Cladosporium*, *Limacinula*, and *Scorias*. The black fungus forms large patches on the leaves and may serious affect photosynthesis, which in turn can have a major impact upon fruit yield and the general health of the plant.

Citrus Canker

Canker disease is a serious problem in South America, Southeast Asia, and Florida. Caused by the bacterium *Xanthomonas campestris* pv. *citri*, it occurs in hot countries and spreads during wet and windy weather. The disease causes spots on leaves and fruit, while serious attacks cause defoliation and the premature loss of fruit. Plants can be protected to some extent by using the copper-based Bordeaux mixture and by erecting windbreaks to limit the spread of the disease.

The United States successfully eradicated citrus canker in Florida during the 1910s and 1980s. A further attempt was made in the 1990s, but this failed after Hurricane Wilma spread the disease throughout the state in 2005. Citrus canker is now so widespread in Florida that it is considered to be impossible to eradicate it. New legislation has imposed a quarantine on the entire state of Florida, in the hope that this disease can be prevented from spreading to the other citrus-producing areas of the United States. Neither trees nor fruit can be exported from Florida to other parts of the United States. The new law obliges Florida citrus nurseries to grow all of their young plants indoors rather than in open fields.

Phytophthora

Phytophthora is one of the most damaging diseases of citrus, causing damping-off disease in seedlings, foot rot, fibrous root rot, and gummosis in mature plants. It is present in most orange groves and is a natural pathogen, rather than having been imported from elsewhere. The disease is caused by several species of *Phytophthora*, but the most dangerous are *P. citrophthora* and *P. nicotiana* var. *parasitica*.

Foot rot starts as an infection of the scion and spreads down to the graft union. Lesions appear around the stem and the leaves eventually turn pale and have yellow veins. The spots become larger and the tree starts to exude a gum. Fibrous root rot affects the cortex of the roots, which turn brown and die. Infected trees lose vitality, the leaves fall off, and the plant suffers from dieback. Trifoliate orange (*Poncirus trifoliata*) appears to be largely unaffected by phytophthora; sour orange (*Citrus aurantium*) and 'Carrizo' citrange are tolerant of foot rot, but succumb to root rot. 'Cleopatra' mandarin and Volkamer lemon are susceptible to both foot and root rot.

The disease is easily spread on weakened plants or soil. Good sanitation is obviously essential. New orchards should, if possible, be planted on land that has not been previously used for growing citrus trees and disease-free plants should be used. Phytophthora is controlled using the systemic fungicides metalaxyl and fosetyl-al, but the chemicals have to be alternated to prevent resistance building up.

Containerised plants can also suffer from phytophthora. If you suspect that a plant is infected it is better to destroy it and dispose of the soil, rather than risk infecting other parts of your garden. Always used sterilised compost when you are potting-on a citrus tree and, wherever possible, a new pot.

Citrus Greening (Yellow Dragon Disease)

Citrus greening is a serious condition in Southeast Asia and southern Africa. Infested trees develop chlorosis and have very small fruit. The disease is caused by the bacterium *Candidatus Liberibacter asiaticus*. (To be validly described bacteria have to be isolated and maintained in culture. Where this is not possible, but the organism can be described, it is given indefinite rank and the prefix *Candidatus* in italic letters.) The disease is spread by the Asian citrus psyllid (*Diaphorina citri*), which feeds on the sap of the tree, or by using contaminated grafting tools and secateurs. Citrus greening can be killed with an anti-biotic (Samson 1980), but none of the available rootstocks are resistant to the bacterium.

Citrus Scab

Citrus scab is caused by the fungus *Elsinoe fawcetii*. Infected plants have distorted shoots and warty growths on the leaves and fruit. The warts eventually coalesce and cause the fruit to crack. The disease is spread by persistent rain and overhead irrigation, but can be reduced by spraying with fungicides.

Citrus Tristeza Virus (CTV)

Tristeza is by far the most serious disease of citrus and has caused the death of millions of trees since it was first recognised in the 1930s. The name means 'misery' or 'unhappiness' in Spanish. The disease probably originated from Asia, where local citrus cultivars are resistant.

The first cultivated citrus trees in the West were grown from seed and were thus free of the disease, but they proved to be vulnerable to phytophthora and were subsequently grafted onto a sour orange rootstock. CTV was first found in Florida during the 1950s and killed many of the trees that were grafted onto a sour orange or *Citrus macrophylla* rootstock. The virus kills the phloem in the rootstock and effectively deprives the scion of nutrition and water. The first sign of infection is the production of smaller leaves and twig dieback.

CTV is spread by aphids, which pass the disease from tree to tree as they feed on the sap. The most virulent strains of the virus can kill a tree within a few weeks, while the less aggressive affect the vigour of the tree, resulting in a crop of very small fruit. Sweet oranges are most seriously affected, followed by limes and grapefruit. Lemons are resistant.

Quarantine is the only effective control for this disease; chemical and biological methods do not work because plants are usually infected before insecticides or beneficial insects can kill the aphids. Florida has spent millions of dollars trying to eradicate the disease, which has devastated the state's citrus crop. The disease has proved almost impossible to control because citrus trees are widely grown as garden plants in Florida. Millions of trees have been uprooted and replaced with fresh, virus-free stock only to be re-infected a few months later.

Although tristeza is unlikely to be an issue in a cold, temperate climate, where the most likely problem will be scale insects, you should be aware that your plants could already harbour the disease and under no circumstances should you take cuttings or fruit to a country that grows citrus as a commercial crop. Virus-free budwood is produced from trees that are grown in sealed, aphid-proof glasshouses, which incorporate a number of safety features. Access to these sites is strictly controlled to reduce the likelihood of the disease being introduced by error. Citrus budwood can be exported to other countries, but it has to be done under very strict supervision. Some nurseries, such as Global Orange Groves in the United Kingdom, supply citrus trees that are certified as being grown on a virus-free rootstock. The origin of the tree, its certification, and the nature of the scion and the rootstock are detailed on a label, which is attached to the tree. It is not essential to have certified material if you live in a cool temperate climate because there are no commercial orchards to infect, but it is reassuring. Citrus trees are very attractive to aphids and they can transmit viruses from one tree to another.

There are a number of simple guidelines that you can follow to avoid spreading citrus viruses:

- Do not propagate plants from potentially diseased material.
- Do not take knives and secateurs to citrus collections.
- Dip knives and secateurs in bleach for a couple of minutes before you use them.
- Do not import plants from other countries. Mal secco and xyloporosis are common in Mediterranean citrus orchards. Holidaymakers often smuggle plants through customs in their luggage.
- Do not import fruit. It can harbour fruit flies, which can also transmit the disease to living fruit trees.
- Don't forget that even home-grown trees can harbour diseases.

Citrus Exocortis Disease (CEVd)

Exocortis is caused by a viroid—an infectious piece of RNA that is smaller than a true virus. The organism causes stunting and affects yields, but has little affect upon the quality of the fruit. Viroids are usually transmitted by infected budwood, but they can also be transferred on infected secateurs and grafting knives. Trifoliate orange and its hybrids, such as citranges, are very sensitive to CEVd. There is no cure for exocortis and budwood should always be obtained from a nursery that is certified to be free of the disease.

Xyloporosis (Citrus Cachexia Viroid)

Xyloporosis is a serious problem in the countries surrounding the Mediterranean Sea. The disease, which is caused by the citrus cachexia viroid and spread by grafting with infected budwood, causes severe damage to mandarins, but no symptoms in sweet oranges, grapefruit, or lemons. The bark becomes discoloured and later splits, producing a general decline in the host and a drop in fruit yields. There is no cure for the disease, but it can be prevented by using certified, virus-free budwood. Sour orange is resistant to the disease.

Mal Secco (Drying Disease)

Mal secco (*Deuterophoma tracheiphila*, synonym *Phoma tracheiphila*) is a serious disease in the countries surrounding the Mediterranean basin, parts of Africa, and around the Black Sea. The disease is caused by a fungus and seriously affects lemons and citrons, causing chlorosis and eventually leaf loss. It can also infect mandarins, sour orange, bergamot, and limes, but sweet oranges and grapefruit are less susceptible. The disease is spread by rain and overhead irrigation. It can be controlled by using chemical fungicides or the copper-based Bordeaux mixture. Volkamer lemon is often used as a rootstock for lemons in Italy, because it is highly resistant to mal secco.

Nematodes

Nematodes are extremely small un-segmented worms that live in the soil. They measure approximately 1 millimetre (3/64 in.) long. While many of them are beneficial, a few are not.

Slow Decline

Citrus trees infected with the citrus nematode (*Tylenchulus semipenetrans*) suffer from reduced vigour, yellow foliage, and smaller-than-usual fruit. There is no cure for the disease, but the arrival of nematodes can be delayed by planting trees on fresh land that has not been used for growing citrus trees. The new trees should be purchased from a respected nursery that can guarantee nematode-free stock. 'Carrizo' and 'Troyer' citranges are being increasingly used as a citrus rootstock because they have natural resistance to the citrus nematode.

Spreading Decline

The burrowing nematode (*Radopholus similes*) attacks the roots of citrus trees and causes infected trees to wilt in hot weather. 'Milam' rough lemon and 'Carrizo' citrange show good tolerance to the nematode.

Insect Pests

The most serious pest in cold climates is likely to be scale insects, which are almost impossible to eradicate once they have become established. Newly purchased plants should be strictly quarantined because this is the most likely route for the introduction of new pests and diseases. Always buy your citrus trees from an established nursery and check them when you get home.

If you must use an insecticide to control a pest, remember that most insecticides are lethal to bees and should not be used when plants are flowering. This rule can be difficult to follow when growing lemons, which often flower throughout the year. If an insecticide is necessary, always spray your plants on a calm day, when there is less of a risk of the spray drifting across other plants or into your neighbour's garden.

▲ The rough lemon 'Milam' is not only resistant to spreading decline disease, but it also produces very vigorous trees with plenty of fruit.

Citrus Whitefly (*Dialeurodes citri*)

The citrus whitefly is a serious pest of citrus in Florida and was introduced from India in the middle of the nineteenth century. It is a small, light-orange coloured insect measuring approximately 3 millimetres (1/8 in.) long, with four wax-covered wings. The larvae feed on the plant's sap and exude honeydew, which is then colonised by sooty mould fungus. The black mould interferes with photosynthesis, leaving the trees weakened and unable to produce a normal yield of fruit. The pest has been controlled in Florida by using a parasitic wasp (*Encarsia lahorensis*), which has greatly reduced the whitefly populations. The whitefly is often controlled by naturally occurring fungi, but these are reduced if the plants are sprayed with copper-based fungicides.

Citrus Blackfly (*Aleurocanthus woglumi*)

The citrus blackfly is a native of Asia, but has spread to Florida via Jamaica, Cuba, and Mexico. The larvae feed on the sap of the citrus tree and exude honeydew, which is colonised by sooty mould. The black mould inhibits photosynthesis and reduces fruit yields. The fly is controlled by two parasitic wasps *Encarsia opulenta* and *Amitus hesperidium*.

Citrus Mealy Bug (*Planococcus citri*)

The citrus mealy bug is a small insect with two wings, measuring approximately 3 mm (1/8 in.) long. The female insect lays its eggs in a white cottony mass. The pupae feed on the sap of the citrus plants and exude honeydew, which is colonised by sooty mould fungus. The larvae cause discoloured fruit and a bumpy or scarred surface. Severe attacks often result in defoliation. Three types of biological control are available: the ladybird beetle (*Cryptolaemus montrouzieri*), an insect parasite (*Leptomastidae abnormis*), and a fungus (*Entomophthora fumosa*). Alternatively, the insecticide imidacloprid (the main ingredient in Bayer's Provado Ultimate Bug Killer) can be used.

Cottony Cushion Scale (*Icerya purchasi*)

The cottony cushion scale is a native of Australia and first found its way to California in the late 1860s. It caused serious damage there and eventually spread to Florida and the rest of the citrus-growing countries of the world. The insects look very different from other scale insects. Their bodies are red, yellow, or brown and covered with a white or yellowish wax coating. Young nymphs settle along the mid rib of the leaf and, when mature, on other parts of the tree. Infected plants often lose their leaves or become covered with sooty mould fungus. Most scale insects are impervious to insecticides when they are mature and must be tackled when they are at the mobile crawler stage. Mature scale insects can be controlled on backyard plants by removing the adults with a piece of cotton wool soaked with methylated spirits and then spraying the plant with imidacloprid (Provado Ultimate Bug Killer in the United Kingdom, Admire in the United States) to kill the crawlers.

Citrus Leaf Miner (*Phyllocnistis citrella*)

The citrus leaf miner originated from Asia, but has now spread to most citrus-growing parts of the world. The larvae burrow into the young leaves of citrus plants and leave serpentine trails in the upper and lower surfaces. This pest can be controlled by imidacloprid (Admire) or abamectin (Syngenta's Agri-Mek).

Citrus Rust Mite (*Phyllocoptruta oleivora*)

A serious pest in Florida, Texas, and parts of California, this mite is very small, measuring approximately 0.1 mm long. It causes the leaves to lose their glossy colour. Infected fruit are covered with light brown or black spots, which makes them difficult to sell. Wettable sulphur provides good control and has the benefit of being non-toxic.

Red Citrus Mite (*Panonychus citri*)

The red citrus mite is a major pest in Florida and California and causes severe damage to the tree's foliage. The infected plant loses vitality and often drops its foliage. It can be controlled with *Amblyseius hibisci*, a predator mite (Davidson and Lyon 1979).

Scale Insects

This interesting group of insects includes several thousand species which can be divided into three main types: soft scale, armoured scale, and mealy bug. The armoured scale is usually the most problematical, with the female adult spending its life permanently fixed to the host plant. The male, by contrast, is an active fly with a single pair of wings and only lives for a few days.

Scale insects are a persistent pest of citrus and can severely weaken a plant if they are not controlled. The immature stage of the female insect, the crawler, is mobile and eventually attaches itself to the midrib of the leaf or along the young shoots, where it feeds on the sap of the plant. The female exudes a waxy covering, the scale, which protects it from predators. The eggs are produced under the scale and eventually hatch to produce more crawlers. The scale insect exudes honeydew, which is then colonised by black mould.

The hard convex shell protects the pest from predators and makes it very difficult to eradicate. Small numbers of scale insects can be removed by rubbing them off with a piece of cotton wool that has been soaked in methylated spirits (methanol). Until recently I would have recommended the organophosphate Malathion (Maldison in Australia and New Zealand and Mercaptothion in South Africa) as a foolproof way of controlling scale insects. However, recent changes in European legislation have led to many long-established insecticides being withdrawn from the market in the European Union. Imidacloprid (sold by Bayer as Provado Ultimate Bug Killer in the United Kingdom and Admire in the United States) is currently the only insecticide that is readily available for the control of scale insects.

Biological control can be achieved by using the parasitic wasp *Metaphycus helvolus*, but this is only effective when the plants are being grown indoors. Scale insects are less of a problem when citrus are grown outside, presumably because there are a number of natural predators that prey on them. The pest is very difficult to eradicate unless you are willing to spray the plants on a regular basis.

Temperate Climate Pests

Gardeners in temperate climates rarely experience the problems that citrus growers have in hotter climes. Nevertheless, the pests and diseases can be irritating and must be tackled. They rarely kill a plant but may disfigure it and reduce its vigour.

Anyone who collects a group of plants will acquire a number of pests and diseases along the way. Some European nurseries are less careful than they should be and sometimes sell plants that are infested with scale insects. They are very difficult to eradicate and it is worth carefully inspecting potential acquisitions before you buy them. Don't be fobbed off by claims that they were recently sprayed; just walk away and find another supplier who takes more care over the health of his or her citrus plants. It is always a good idea to quarantine a new acquisition before it is added to an established collection, because once you have scale insects it is unlikely that you'll ever get rid of them completely.

Ants

While ants rarely cause direct damage to a citrus tree, they must be controlled

▲ Scale insects are a serious pest of citrus fruit and can weaken a tree if they are not controlled. They are difficult to eradicate when established.

if scale insects are present. Ants protect scale insects from predators and parasites and feed off the honeydew that the scale insects exude. They rarely damage a plant directly, but may cause the plant to wilt during hot weather if they establish a nest in the pot. Ant powder, which usually incorporates permethrin as the active ingredient, is quite effective against these ubiquitous insects.

In a commercial orchard, ants perform a useful function by controlling the number of pests that overwinter as pupae in the soil. Thus, although commercial orchards can use an insecticide to control them, the ants are usually controlled by placing ant bands around the trunk of the tree. These collars are coated with a sticky substance, which prevents the ants from reaching the other parts of the tree.

Aphids

Aphids are rarely a serious problem in a cool temperate climate, but they can distort the growth of young buds and may need to be controlled. They exude honeydew, which encourages the development of sooty moulds and can pass viruses from one tree to another. The black citrus aphid (*Toxoptera citricidus*) is the most feared because it transmits the citrus tristeza virus.

Mice

Citrus bark provides an attractive source of food for starving mice, and the rodents can become a problem for people who grow their plants in a cold temperate climate. Mice eat the bark of younger twigs, which, if not controlled, may cause severe damage. Rodents rarely kill a tree but it may suffer a serious setback and will take some time to recover. The damaged branches should be removed in the spring with a pair of secateurs, and the plant will produce new foliage. Watering should be limited until the plant has developed a good canopy of leaves. Mice should not be allowed to damage a tree in two consecutive years. Mature citrus are pretty tough, but they will not tolerate two consecutive years of damage.

Vine Weevils (*Otiorhynchus sulcatus*)

The damage caused by vine weevils is often underestimated because the larvae spend all of their lives underground eating the roots of host plants and are rarely seen. These pernicious pests rarely kill citrus trees, but can weaken them and render them more vulnerable to pathogens or pathogenic organisms. The adult beetles are quite distinctive and can sometimes be found on the walls of buildings, while the dead larvae may be found in plant saucers if a citrus tree has been watered and the excess water is allowed to stand for more than an hour (this practice is not recommended because the excess water may damage the tree's roots). The adults feed on the foliage and leave characteristic notches on the leaf margin.

Most home gardeners who grow citrus obviously look forward to the day when they can eat fruit from their own trees and are worried about the idea of using chemical insecticides. Biological forms of control such as Becker Underwood's aptly named Nemasys H are just as effective and remove the risk of eating organophosphate residues. Nemasys H uses a pathogenic nematode (*Heterorhabditis megidis*), which penetrates the body of the vine weevil larva and releases bacteria, which in turn kill the pest. Nemasys L was developed by Horticultural Research International in the United Kingdom and can be used at lower temperatures than Nemasys H. It uses a different nematode (*Steinernema kraussei*) and is also distributed by Becker Underwood.

Greenhouse Red Spider Mite (*Tetranychus urticae*)

This ubiquitous insect can be a major problem for plants in a heated greenhouse or conservatory. These mites cause damage by puncturing the cells of the leaf with their proboscis and then feeding on its contents. Red spider mites are resistant to several insecticides, but can be controlled by spraying the foliage with water in the evening and by maintaining a higher humidity.

Snails

Snails may cause a significant amount of damage to citrus trees in the spring, but are relatively easy to control. A piece of copper foil wrapped around the trunk of the tree will deter both slugs and snails. Using copper is preferable to using metaldehyde, which will also kill beneficial organisms such as frogs.

◀ Carnation tortrix moth (*Cacoecimorpha pronubana*) can cause serious damage to citrus plants. The caterpillars protect themselves by drawing the young leaves together with silk-like threads, distorting the leaves in the process. The caterpillars then eat the leaves.

▲ Female tortrix moths lay their eggs on the underside of citrus leaves. The larvae initially feed in the area and then spread around the rest of the tree, where they can cause considerable damage. They can be controlled by using a pheromone trap.

Carnation Tortrix Moth (*Cacoecimorpha pronubana*)

Also known as the European carnation moth, this voracious caterpillar can cause serious damage to citrus trees and in my experience is extremely difficult to eradicate. The insects are quite small, rarely measuring more than 12 millimetres (½ in.) long. Tortrix moth larvae feed on the leaves during the early summer and draw them together by spinning silk. These pests are quite difficult to detect, but when the leaves are pulled apart the distinctive green caterpillars move quickly backwards in a characteristic arching manner. The young caterpillars feed for approximately one month and then wrap themselves in a silk cocoon, where they pupate. The small, dark brown pupae measure approximately 9–12 millimetres (a little less than ½ in.) long and can sometimes be found lying on the surface of the compost or on the ground around the citrus pots. Rest assured, they are not butterflies and should be destroyed as soon as possible.

The female adults emerge in the spring and fly at dusk or sunrise, laying eggs on the underside of the leaves. When the larvae emerge they feed on the leaf in the immediate vicinity of the hatching site and then migrate to the young, growing shoots of the tree. If you can find the area where the eggs have been laid, you can greatly reduce the potential damage by destroying the caterpillars before they have had a chance to migrate to other areas of the tree. Young, recently hatched caterpillars are sensitive to light and can be found underneath the citrus leaf. Be careful not to disturb the caterpillars because they will fall off and descend to the ground on a thin thread of silk. Older caterpillars are very mobile and it's a good idea to place a container underneath when you are prising the leaves apart.

Tortrix moths cause serious damage to several other fruit trees, but whereas apples and cherries are deciduous and shed their leaves in the autumn, citrus bear their scars until the leaves fall off between two and three years later. The moths usually produce at least two to three new generations per year, and the caterpillars can remain active during the winter if the plants are kept in a heated conservatory. The adult larvae feed on the upper surface of the leaf and leave irregular brown patches, as well as distorting the growth of young buds. They cause a disproportionate amount of damage for their small size and must be controlled. It is often better to remove damaged shoots than allow them to develop into unsightly leaves. A vigorous tree will probably produce new shoots to replace the lost ones.

I have tried several ways to control tortrix moths, but pheromone traps appear to be the most successful method. Male moths are attracted to a lure within the trap and become stuck in the sticky surface. Without any males the female moth is unable to produce any fertile eggs and in theory your plants should be less vulnerable to attack. The trap seems to attract male moths from some distance away, but will not prevent a previously impregnated female from laying eggs on your citrus plant. It is easy to underestimate how many tortrix moths are present in an area and you may surprised to find how many male moths are attracted to your pheromone trap. I once set up a trap above a 'Star Ruby' grapefruit plant and caught 30 male moths within 36 hours. The adults are quite small and inconspicuous and you may not see them unless you are actually watching your citrus trees.

Biological control can never be completely effective if your citrus trees are being grown outside. If the pheromone trap is attracting a lot of male moths, it safe to assume that there are a large number of female moths around as well and that a proportion of them will already have fertilised eggs. I never feel entirely happy resorting to chemicals, but with some pests you really have little choice. The best insecticides to use against the caterpillars are those based on derris and bifenthrin. Both of these are extremely dangerous to bees and should not be applied to flowering trees or on windy days. If some of your trees are flowering, mark them carefully and move them away from the area where you are spraying. If the damage is very bad it is possible to remove the flowers beforehand, but this would probably prevent the trees from carrying any fruit later that year. Derris and bifenthrin are relatively safe to use around children and pets, but are highly toxic to fish.

Tortrix moths are remarkably resistant to organophosphate insecticide, which will control pernicious pests such as scale insects; tortrix moth caterpillars still survive after a tree has been completely drenched in the chemical. The only effective way of controlling them is to separate every leaf on the tree and inspect it for green caterpillars. The damage from tortrix moth larvae may not show for several weeks, by which time the damage has been done.

▲ 'Biondo Comune', an old sweet orange cultivar from Italy, is still widely cultivated in that country.

8 An Encyclopedia of Citrus

Citrus trees have been cultivated in the West for more than four hundred years and during this time several thousand cultivars have been introduced. To this number can be added the many cultivars that have been raised in Southeast Asia and several closely related species with decorative merit. Very few of these cultivars have ever succeeded commercially and the same citrus variety may have several synonyms, depending upon where it is growing. In some countries it is quite common to come across older cultivars that have been superseded by better plants elsewhere, but are retained because they are well adapted to the local area. Many of these are raised from seed and are called common oranges or lemons. While these plants can rarely compete with the better-established cultivars, they form a valuable gene pool for future breeding.

It would be impossible to cover all of these plants within the confines of this book. Only a limited number of citrus trees are readily available from nurseries and garden centres and I have concentrated on describing these.

A quick glimpse of the taxonomic arrangement of citrus in Webber and Batchelor (1943) will reveal the complexity of citrus taxonomy. Many of the species named in the past are actually hybrids and have few morphological differences to distinguish them. To make matters worse, some older citrus cultivars have been given different names in various parts of the world. It is only now that horticulturalists realise the names actually apply to the same plant. The 'correct' name is selected according to the rules outlined in the *International Code for the Nomenclature of Cultivated Plants* (2004).

The following descriptions are based upon my own observations and published material about the different citrus varieties. The fact that a plant is no longer grown commercially does not mean that it is unsuitable for growing at home. Plants often have other traits, such as attractive foliage, cold hardiness, or the absence of thorns, that make them good ornamentals.

Specialist nurseries will be able to give you guidance, based upon their experience of growing these plants for many years.

Sweet Orange (*Citrus sinensis*)

There are four types of cultivated oranges. These are the common or blonde orange, the sugar orange, the blood orange, and the navel orange. 'Washington' navel and 'Valencia' are by far the most widely grown sweet orange cultivars and are readily available from nurseries.

Common Oranges

The term *common orange* refers to the many thousands of different seed-raised plants that are grown in citrus-producing countries. Common oranges tend to be well adapted to the region where they are growing, but produce rather thorny trees and bear somewhat indifferent fruit. They are known as *comuna* in Spain, *comune* in Italy, *beladi* in North Africa, and *criolla* in Argentina and Uruguay. Seed-raised plants have varying tolerance to disease and are gradually being replaced by named cultivars on good-quality rootstocks. Common oranges are often seen on sale in the markets of Mediterranean countries and sometimes find their way into supermarkets. The term is confusing because it is sometimes attached to named cultivars.

Home gardeners should always buy a named variety of citrus tree and never one that is only marked with the species name, such as *Citrus limon*, or a local vernacular name, such as *naranja* (Spanish for orange). In most cases the plant will be a well-respected cultivar, but there is no way of knowing. There is little point in waiting for ten years while your citrus tree grows to a reasonable size, only to find that it produces inferior fruit.

'Biondo Comune'
'Biondo Comune' is one of the oldest Italian cultivars of sweet orange, but is rarely planted now and will eventually die out. The trees are very vigorous and produce medium-sized, very juicy, yellowish-orange fruit. This orange is still common in smaller orchards.

'Salustiana'
'Salustiana' orange has pleasantly flavoured fruit, with a lingering bitterness and very few, if any, seeds. The fruit are reasonably easy to peel,

but tend to leave a layer of mesocarp around the segments. Widely grown in Spain, 'Salustiana' arose as a bud mutation on a 'Commune' orange in 1950. It was named after its propagator, Don Salustiano Pallas (Saunt 1990). The fruit fill an important gap in the market, because they can be harvested several weeks before 'Valencia' fruit. Mature fruit can be left on the tree for some time, with little deterioration.

'Shamouti'

'Shamouti' (synonym 'Jaffa') orange is very easy to peel and has an excellent flavour, making it a good dessert fruit. Unfortunately, it doesn't produce very much juice and it suffers from delayed bitterness, which makes it unsuitable for commercial juice production. This cultivar has been grown in Israel for more than 160 years and used to be the most widely grown sweet orange in the Eastern Mediterranean; however, it is sensitive to very hot weather and arid conditions and is now mainly grown along the Western coast of Israel and on the island of Cyprus. The deep orange fruit have a distinctive oval shape with a thick, rather pitted peel and very few seeds. Webber and Batchelor (1943) treated 'Jaffa' orange as a separate cultivar, but they are now considered to be identical. The trees are moderately vigorous and grow particularly well on a Volkamer lemon rootstock. 'Shamouti' is prone to producing bud sports and several selections are in cultivation. The fruit store well.

◄◄ 'Shamouti' was once the most widely grown sweet orange in the Eastern Mediterranean. Today it is mainly grown in Israel and Cyprus.

◄ The flavourful fruit of 'Shamouti' has a distinctive oval shape with a thick, rather pitted peel and very few seeds.

◁ 'Valencia' is the world's most widely grown orange. The fruit mature later than most other sweet oranges.

▷ 'Cutter' is an improved form of 'Valencia' orange. The trees are more vigorous and productive than those of 'Valencia'.

'Valencia'

'Valencia' (synonyms 'Hart's Late', 'Hart's Tardiff', 'Rivers' Late', 'Valencia Late') is a late-ripening orange, with sweet, juicy fruit and a relatively thin skin. It is by far the most widely grown orange in the world and the leading cultivar in many citrus-growing countries. The trees are very vigorous, with spherical to oval, medium-sized, deep reddish-orange fruit, which can be left on the tree for a long time, but are usually harvested in the spring. 'Valencia' is one of the latest sweet oranges to appear on supermarket shelves. The fruit provides the majority of Florida's orange juice.

'Valencia' oranges aren't as easy to peel as navel oranges, but have very sweet flesh and few seeds. The trees are often alternate bearing; that is, they produce a very good yield in one year, but far less in the subsequent season. This characteristic is more pronounced if the previous year's fruit crop is left on the tree for a prolonged period of time. Although the fruit can be left on the tree until the summer, they are likely to turn green again as chlorophyll develops in the strong sunshine. The fruit is still edible when green.

'Valencia' orange has an interesting history. The American stock of the plant originated in the Azores and was sent to Thomas Rivers III, the owner of a well-established fruit nursery, in Hertfordshire, England. Rivers recognised the potential of the tree and called it 'Excelsior'. The plant was propagated and in 1876 sent to three American growers, one in California and the other two in Florida. The California package arrived without any labels, so the owners called the tree 'Rivers' Late'. The package destined for E. H. Hart in Florida was delivered to Parsons Nursery in New York. By the time the package was forwarded to Hart's, the labels had also fallen off. Hart's tree was submitted to the Florida State Horticultural Society, which gave it the name 'Hart's Tardiff'. The name was subsequently changed to 'Hart's Late'.

In the late nineteenth century it was realised that 'Excelsior' was actually the same as an orange that grew in the area around Valencia in Spain. The orange was subsequently renamed 'Valencia', in recognition of its true origin. Several selections of 'Valencia' orange are in cultivation, including 'Campbell', 'Cutter', 'Delta', 'Frost', and 'Olinda'.

Navel Oranges

Navel oranges are easily recognised because they usually have a conspicuous navel at the bottom of the fruit. If the fruit is cut in half, a second and sometimes a third set of segments can be seen below the main one. The size of the navel varies from fruit to fruit and is sometimes invisible from the outside. 'Washington' navel matures several weeks earlier than 'Valencia' orange and is renowned for its flavour. Several late-maturing cultivars have been raised in Australia since the 1950s and one of these ('Lane Late') has been widely planted in California and Australia. Navel oranges have excellent flavour and are mainly purchased as dessert fruit. Unfortunately, most cultivars have low levels of a bitter-tasting chemical called limonin, which makes them unsuitable for juice production. Navel oranges are less successful in Florida, but thrive in California's cooler climate.

'Cara Cara'

Sometimes known as the pink navel orange, 'Cara Cara' looks wonderful in salads. The external rind is orange like most other navel oranges, but the flesh is a deep reddish pink, somewhat like that of the grapefruit 'Star Ruby'. The deep red colouration, which is caused by the presence of

lycopene and beta-carotene, rather than the antho-cyanins that give blood oranges their distinctive colour, does not need cold weather to develop. Lycopene is an anti-oxidant and is usually found in tomatoes, while beta-carotene occurs in carrots.

'Cara Cara' arose as a limb sport on a 'Washington' navel orange at Hacienda Cara Cara in Venezuela. The plant is genetically unstable and sometimes produces normal fruit with orange rather than red flesh and sometimes has variegated foliage. 'Cara Cara' was first introduced into Florida in 1987. The fruit are seedless, measure approximately 7.5 centimetres (3 in.) across, and can be harvested from December to February.

'Lane Late'

This tasty, late-maturing navel orange has a relatively thin rind and a pleasant balance of acidity and sweetness. Its fruit mature between four and six weeks later than fruit of its parent, the ubiquitous 'Washington' navel, and can be left on the tree for several months without showing much sign of deterioration. The rind is smooth and yellowish orange. 'Lane Late' is extensively grown in Australia. It appeared as a bud mutation in 1950 and was named after its owner. 'Washington' navel is usually harvested from November to December, while 'Lane Late' can be collected from January to March. It has very low levels of limonin, the bitter-tasting chemical that makes most navels unsuitable for juice production.

'Navelina'

'Navelina' (synonyms 'Smith's Early Navel', 'Washington Early') originated as a bud sport from a 'Washington' navel at the Citrus Research Station in Riverside, California. It was originally called 'Smith's Early Navel' and exported to Spain in 1933. After further development it returned to California in 1990. The fruit, which mature several weeks earlier than 'Washington' navel fruit, can be harvested in November, are pear-shaped and usually seedless, but their flavour is not as good as that of the parent and they are slightly smaller with a small navel. The attractive tree is less vigorous and smaller than its parent. It also has no thorns and this makes it a good choice for a conservatory plant. 'Navelina' has been extensively planted in Spain.

'Newhall'

'Newhall' navel originated as a bud sport on 'Washington' and was selected by David Hackney of the Newhall Land and Water Company in California. The tree is smaller and slightly less vigorous than its parent, but the fruit matures earlier and has a deeper reddish-orange rind. 'Newhall' looks very similar to 'Navelina' and is often sold under that name in Spain, where both cultivars have been extensively planted.

'Washington'

'Washington' (synonyms 'Bahia', 'Riverside Navel', 'Washington Navel') navel is arguably the single most important cultivar of sweet orange in existence and is widely grown throughout the world. The bulk of early dessert oranges are 'Washington' navels, and while there are several improved selections, they have made little impact on the popularity of the original plant. 'Washington' was initially thought to have come from Brazil, but recent research suggests that it first appeared in Spain and was subsequently taken to Brazil.

In 1870 twelve of the grafted Brazilian trees were sent to the U.S. Department of Agriculture in Washington, D.C. These were then distributed to interested growers in California and Florida. Three of the young trees were sent to Eliza Tibbetts of Riverside, California, who subsequently won a competition with one of his trees. The 'Washington' navel was soon recognised as being of superior quality and within a decade was the most widely grown cultivar of sweet orange in the area. One of the original trees has survived to the present day and can be found growing in a small park in Riverside.

'Washington' navel proved to be sensitive to high temperatures and arid conditions and was never very successful in Florida; however, it thrived in California and was largely responsible for the success of the state's citrus industry. It ripens several weeks before 'Valencia' and is mainly grown as a dessert fruit.

The fruit of 'Washington' are deep orange, with a slightly pitted surface and a relatively large navel at the base. The navel is usually partially

One of the two original trees from which all Washington Navel oranges in California have descended. Propagated from trees imported from Bahia, Brazil in 1870 by the U.S. Dept. of Agriculture, and sent to Riverside, Cal. in 1873

◁ Visitors to Riverside, California, can visit one of the first 'Washington' navel orange trees to be grown in the United States. The tree is 130 years old and still going strong.

▷ 'Thomson' is a selection of the famous 'Washington' navel orange. Although the fruit matures a fortnight earlier, the tree is less vigorous and it never became a commercial success.

◁ Plaque commemorating the first 'Washington' navel orange tree, Riverside, California.

covered by the rind or may protrude slightly. The fruit are very sweet and have an excellent flavour, are seedless, and have quite a thick skin, which makes them easier to peel.

This reliable plant is a good choice if you only have room to grow one sweet orange tree. It has a small number of thorns. The fruit are harvested from December to April.

'Thomson'

Many new cultivars of citrus have been derived from bud mutations on existing trees, but some of them fail to live up to expectation. 'Thomson' (synonym 'Thomson Improved') is a good example. The plant originated as a bud mutation on a 'Washington' navel in 1891 and was named after the orchard's owner, A. C. Thomson. It was initially well received because the fruit matured a fortnight earlier than its parent. This trait could have given its growers a major commercial advantage, but unfortunately the cultivar turned out to be genetically unstable and the fruit deteriorated quickly after it had ripened. This cultivar was planted in Algeria, Morocco, Chile, and Australia, where the experience has been the same.

Sugar Oranges

The acidless or sweet oranges are a small group of cultivars with high levels of sugar and very little acidity. They are known as *dolce* in Italy, *douce* in France, and 'Sucreña' in Spain. Sweet oranges are unsuitable for juice production and have a rather insipid flavour.

Blood or Pigmented Oranges

Blood oranges are a distinctive group of citrus fruit with red-pigmented, strongly flavoured flesh. Large quantities of them are grown on the foothills of Mount Etna, on the island of Sicily, where they were first cultivated. Since then the plants have been adopted by citrus growers in Algeria, Morocco, Spain, Tunisia, and more recently California. Blood oranges have a very strong, distinctive flavour and are mainly grown as a dessert fruit and for their deep red juice. The juice is very popular in Italy but in less demand in northwestern Europe. Some people claim that blood oranges taste of raspberries.

There are two types of blood oranges. Full blood oranges are deeply pigmented with the colour extending throughout the flesh and ranging from orange with a ruby-red flush, to vermillion and deep ruby-red. Half-blood oranges are less deeply pigmented, with red speckled flesh. Some people find the colour of full-blood oranges rather disturbing because it reminds them of bruised flesh and this must have had an impact on the fruit's popularity.

The unusual colour is caused by the presence of red pigments called anthocyanins, which occur widely in the plant kingdom. These pigments are the reason why flowers are red and autumn leaves produce a kaleidoscope of colours in the fall. Anthocyanins only develop in cold weather, however, and blood oranges need low temperatures during the night before they develop their distinctive flavour. The exterior and internal colours vary considerably between cultivars; some have normal orange rind, while others are flushed with red pigment. The pigments are different from those found in the 'Cara Cara' navel orange. The earliest blood orange is reputed as having come from Sicily.

The famous British botanist William Hooker (1834), writing in the early

▲ Malta blood oranges are extensively grown in Tunisia. The fruit are smaller than those of 'Valencia' and navel oranges, but have an excellent flavour.

nineteenth century, described the Malta orange as being one of the best grown on Sicily: 'That named Aranciu di Malta, or Aranciu Sanguignu, the blood red, or Malta Orange, is one of the best and of the sweetest flavour'. This is presumed to be the 'Maltaise Sanguine', a very sweet, half-blood orange, which is still grown on the island.

'Maltaise Sanguine'

'Maltaise Sanguine' (synonyms 'Maltaise de Tunisie', 'Portugaise') is an old cultivar and, as the name suggests, probably originated on the island of Malta. The tree is moderately vigorous and inclined to be alternate bearing. It needs high temperatures to produce good quality fruit and is mainly grown in Tunisia and Morocco where the higher temperatures can be obtained. The medium-sized fruit have a deep orange rind and sweet, very juicy, reddish-orange flesh. They are harvested late in the season, usually between January and February, and have very few seeds. This cultivar is still considered to be one of the best-flavoured oranges. The French refer to it as the queen of oranges. A similar blood orange is grown in Pakistan and in the Punjab in India.

'Moro'

'Moro' blood orange is the most deeply pigmented blood orange and is widely planted in its native Italy. The fruit may be deep orange or flushed with varying amounts of red pigment. The external colour only develops after cold weather. The round or oval fruit are easily peeled and are usually seedless, but at 6 to 7 centimetres (2½–3 in.) across are considerably smaller than navel oranges. The moderately vigorous trees are very decorative and, depending upon the weather, may have normal orange-coloured fruit and deep red fruit at the same time.

'Moro' fruit are best harvested from January to February, after which the skin becomes rather leathery and the quality deteriorates. This cultivar has been successful in California, where the necessary combination of hot summers and cold winter evenings can be obtained.

'Sanguinello'

'Sanguinello' (synonym 'Sanguinello Commune') blood orange is an old, late-maturing variety from Sicily with rather large fruit and a thick, easily peeled skin. The segments are easily separated and reveal a heavily pigmented, wonderfully flavoured flesh, with very few seeds. The fruit, which

Blood oranges are highly sought after in Italy. 'Moro' has deep red flesh.

are harvested from February to March and are used to produce a sweet, deep red fruit juice, look superficially like a navel, with orange or red-flushed skin. Strongly pigmented fruit have the strongest flavour, while those with orange flesh taste much the same as any other orange. The fruit keep well on the tree and can still be harvested in May.

'Spanish Sanguinelli'

The 'Spanish Sanguinelli' (synonyms 'Sanguinelli', 'Sanguinelli Negro') blood orange originated in Spain, where it was found growing as a bud mutation on a 'Doble Fina' orange in 1929. It is a late-ripening variety with bright, reddish-orange, egg-shaped fruit. The thick skin is harder to peel than 'Moro', but the fruit have good flavour and sweet cherry-red flesh. Most of the pigmentation is concentrated beside the segment walls, which gives the cut fruit a distinctive appearance. The outer skin is often deeply pigmented.

'Tarocco'

These wonderfully flavoured, half-blood oranges are extremely popular in Italy and have the highest vitamin C levels of any citrus fruit. The fruit, which have a distinctive collar and can look superficially like a 'Minneola', are yellowish orange on the outside, becoming red flushed as they ripen. There are very few, if any, seeds. The flesh is usually deep orange with speckles of ruby-red when first cut and has an extremely sweet, slightly spicy flavour. I find the flavour and appearance of the cut fruit far superior to that of 'Moro', but this is probably a matter of taste.

'Tarocco' fruit ripen several weeks later than 'Moro' fruit and are usually harvested from late January to early March in central California and a month or so later on the coast. This cultivar is rarely grown in Florida or Texas because the evenings are too warm to allow the fruit to develop its characteristic red pigmentation. Selections include 'Tarocco del Franco-fonte', 'Tarocco del Muso', and 'Tarocco Rosso'. The fruit are the largest of the blood oranges, but deteriorate if they are left on the tree for too long.

Mandarins

Mandarins comprise an extremely complex group of citrus and have been split into at least four species, namely, Mediterranean mandarin (*Citrus deliciosa*), king mandarin (*C. nobilis*), common mandarin (*C. reticulata*), and Satsuma (*C. unshiu*). However, recent research on their DNA suggests

▲ 'Tarocco' is a very sweet-tasting blood orange and has the highest vitamin C levels of any citrus fruit.

that all mandarins actually belong to a single species and their variation is entirely the result of centuries of hybridisation and selection by mankind.

While the common mandarin and the Satsuma appear to be quite different, they are actually closely related to one another. The Satsuma has been grown in Japan for at least four hundred years and during this time it has become quite distinct from its ancestor, both in its hardiness and in the flavour of its fruit. Tangerines have a reddish-orange skin, but are otherwise identical to common mandarins.

Mandarins are usually available from January to March in the Northern Hemisphere and vary considerably in quality. The differences are almost entirely due to subtle variations in the blend of aromatic chemicals in the rind and juice of the fruit. Some cultivars are easier to peel than others and are consequently more popular with the consumer. Many mandarins produce seedless fruit, particularly if they are grown in isolation from other cultivars, while others produce rather seedy fruit. It is worth checking the label on fruit to ensure that you buy the best varieties. Almost all the mandarins in British supermarkets originate from Spain, where 'Nules', 'Fortune', and 'Nova' (under the name 'Clemenvilla') are among the most widely grown varieties.

Mediterranean Mandarin (*Citrus deliciosa*)

The plant that we now know as the Mediterranean mandarin first reached Europe in 1805, when Sir Abraham Hume imported two cultivars of *Citrus deliciosa* from China. The plants were subsequently illustrated in the *Botanical Register* (Edwards 1817) and *The Botanist's Repository* (Andrews 1824). A few years later the British sent grafted trees to the island of Malta, which was one of their colonies, and from there the mandarin subsequently spread to other Mediterranean countries. Several improved cultivars have been produced in Italy.

The trees of Mediterranean mandarin are less vigorous than those of the common mandarin, but have attractive weeping branches, densely covered with small, fragrant, lance-shaped leaves. The plant is quite cold tolerant, but produces rather small, yellowish-orange fruit measuring approximately 5 centimetres (2 in.) in diameter. The fruit have a rather loose, puffy skin, several large seeds, and do not store very well.

Mediterranean mandarin used to be a common sight in European shops but has been largely superseded by the Satsuma and clementine. The fruit have a distinctive fragrance used to produce perfume, while the leaves and young branches are distilled to produce oil of petitgrain.

King Mandarin (*Citrus nobilis*)

The king mandarin, also known as the Indochinese mandarin, Cambodian mandarin, and yellow king mandarin, probably originated in Indochina and was then taken to Japan and China. It is thought to be a natural tangor and has the largest fruit of any mandarin, with an easily peeled skin. The fruit are yellowish orange to orange, oblate or spherical, and often have a large depression in the base. The rind is very thick and uneven, and has conspicuous oil glands. King mandarins need plenty of heat and will not survive a frost.

'King'
'King' (synonym 'King of Siam') is the only cultivar of *Citrus nobilis* that is widely grown in the Western world. It originated in Vietnam and was taken to California in 1880 by John Bingham, the American ambassador to Japan. The tree is widely grown in Southeast Asia, but has been less successful in the United States. The fruit are tasty and easily peeled, but also are very easily damaged and this has limited the cultivar's commercial appeal. 'King' is very vigorous, forming a large tree, and has large yellow-orange to orange fruit with a rather rough, thick skin. The fruit are ready to harvest between January and February.

Common Mandarin (*Citrus reticulata*)

The common mandarin is an extremely complex group of cultivars and includes a number of hybrids with other species. The term *clementine* is quite widely used, but there doesn't seem to be any definition of what constitutes this type of mandarin. The same applies to the term *tangerine*; it has become synonymous with the word *mandarin* and consequently causes considerable confusion.

Tangerines

Tangerines were originally grown in Morocco and derive their name from the port of Tangier, from which they were exported around the world.

Technically, however, they are mandarins and, like the Satsuma, gradually developed distinctive characteristics when they were isolated from other types of mandarin. The word *tangerine* originated in the seventeenth century and was used to describe something that came from Tangier. The term is also used to describe something that is bright reddish orange in colour.

Tangerines were once common in European shops but have been largely superseded by satsumas. Although tangerines have a distinctive flavour and attractive, deep orange-red skin, they are let down by the relatively large number of seeds. The fruit have a thin, shiny, easily removed skin and very sweet flesh, but they tend to deteriorate quickly after they are picked.

'Dancy'

'Dancy' (synonym 'Dancy Tangerine') tangerine originated from an orchard in Buena Vista, Florida, and was probably a seedling from a Moroccan plant. It was named after Colonel George Dancy, who introduced it into cultivation in 1871 or 1872 (Webber and Batchelor 1943). 'Dancy' is also known as zipper-skin or kid glove tangerine. It forms a vigorous, erect tree with large, dark green lance-shaped leaves and bears masses of bright, reddish-orange fruit. The fruit are harvested from November to February in California and sold as a seasonal Christmas fruit.

▶ 'Dancy' was the first citrus to be called a tangerine as it was grown in Tangiers. The term is now loosely applied to any reddish-orange mandarin.

Clementines

The clementine is a distinctive type of mandarin and is probably a hybrid between a sweet orange and a Mediterranean mandarin. Tanaka gave it specific status as *Citrus clementina*.

According to tradition, the original clementine was a chance seedling found growing in a bed of over a thousand mandarin siblings at an orphanage in Misserghin, Algeria. The plant was named after Clement Rodier, the person who had originally planted them and, at that time, the director of the orphanage (Trabut 1902). This story has been questioned, however, and some people believe that the plant originated in China and was taken to Algeria.

Clementines need less heat than other mandarins and have been very successful in Spain and several North African countries. The original clementine was harvested during November and December, but the addition of new cultivars has extended this season from October to April. Clementines are very attractive trees with plenty of dark green foliage. The fruit are usually seedless when the trees are grown in isolation from other mandarin cultivars, but become seedy if cross-pollinated. The fruit will become puffy and dry if they are left on the tree beyond harvest time.

Clementines are ideal for growing in containers and, provided that they are kept warm in the winter, they are one of the few citrus that will always produce a good crop of fruit in the British Isles.

'Commune'
'Commune' (synonyms 'Algerian Tangerine', 'Fina') clementine forms a vigorous rounded tree with narrow, lanceolate leaves. It has thorns. The

◀◀ 'Commune' clementine forms a vigorous rounded tree with narrow, lanceolate leaves and produces large quantities of deep orange or reddish fruit with shiny, easily peeled skin and sweet, juicy flesh.

fruit are round to oblate, deep orange or reddish orange, with a shiny, easily peeled skin. 'Commune' is self-incompatible and in the absence of other mandarins will usually produce seedless fruit. The fruit mature early in the season and have very juicy, well-flavoured flesh.

Originating in Algeria, this plant was exported to Spain and is the parent of all modern Spanish clementines. It is still extensively grown in Spain, but has been superseded by the newer cultivars, which have larger fruit and fewer seeds. The trees are very vigorous and produce large quantities of sweet fruit. This cultivar is rarely planted today, but can still be purchased from European nurseries. Some authors treat 'Commune' and 'Fina' as two separate cultivars.

'Ellendale'

'Ellendale' is a late-maturing mandarin, with deep reddish-orange, very sweet, juicy flesh. The original tree was discovered growing as a chance seedling in the Ellendale Orchard, Queensland, Australia. The plant is thought to be a tangor, a hybrid between a sweet orange and a mandarin. It has large fruit, with a very thin, easily peeled skin and readily separated segments. 'Ellendale' grows well on a trifoliate orange or citrange rootstock and is inclined to produce plenty of seeds unless it is grown in a monoculture.

▶ 'Ellendale' mandarin produces abundant large juicy fruit.

'Fortune'

'Fortune' mandarin was raised in California in 1964 and is a hybrid between the original clementine and 'Dancy' tangerine. The fruit is very similar in shape to that of a Satsuma, but has a deep orange skin like a clementine. 'Fortune' has been very successful in Spain, where it is now the second most widely cultivated mandarin. The skin is easily removed and the flesh is very sweet. The fruit are normally seedless when trees are planted in isolation from other cultivars, but become very seedy when cross-pollinated. The vigorous, highly productive trees carry their fruit beneath the foliage, where they are protected from the sun.

◀ 'Fortune' mandarin is a hybrid between the original clementine and 'Dancy' tangerine.

▶ 'Frua' mandarin has wrinkled, Satsuma-like fruit.

'Frua'

'Frua' mandarin forms an upright pear-shaped tree with wrinkled, Satsuma-like fruit. The fruit have a rather sharp flavour and a few small pips. 'Frua' was developed at the University of California, Riverside, and was crossed with a pummelo to produce 'Cocktail Grapefruit'.

'Nova'

'Nova' (synonym 'Clemenvilla') mandarin forms a vigorous-growing tree with rather thorny branches and relatively large, reddish-orange fruit. The

fruit have a tight skin and are initially difficult to peel, but once broken, the skin is easily removed to reveal fragrant, easily separated segments. 'Nova' is usually seedless when grown in isolation from other mandarins, but will develop a few seeds if compatible plants are in the vicinity. It is usually known as 'Clemenvilla' in Spain and is often found for sale under this name in the United Kingdom.

'Nules'

'Nules' (synonyms 'Clemenules', 'De Nules') mandarin is an excellent dessert fruit with a delicate flavour and one of the best mandarins currently available. The original tree appeared as a bud mutation on 'Fina' clementine in 1953 and has slightly larger fruit than its parent. 'Nules' has been widely planted in Spain and has proved very popular with European con-

sumers. The fruit are seedless and can be harvested from late November to the end of January. Almost spherical, they have a slight depression at the stylar end and a rather pitted surface. They are easy to peel and have juicy, easily separated segments. Children love them.

'Ortanique'

'Ortanique' (synonyms 'Australique', 'Mandora', 'Tambor', 'Topaz') looks like a flattened clementine, but is actually like a natural tangor. No, it's not named after an exotic Caribbean island, but is a combination of three words, namely, ORange, TANgerine, and unIQUE. The skin of the fruit is quite difficult to remove, but after a bit of work and a mouthful of citrus oil, the bare flesh is revealed. The segments are easily separated and have a very rich flavour. The fruit are seedless when the trees are grown in a monoculture, but very seedy when other compatible citrus plants are around.

Originating in Jamaica, 'Ortanique' forms a large, vigorous, almost thornless tree. The fruit are harvested in February and can be left on the tree for several weeks without any significant deterioration. The name was originally trademarked and this explains the large number of alternative names.

Satsuma Mandarin (*Citrus unshiu*)

Children love satsumas and the fruit are the ideal packed-lunch accompaniment: they make a sweet, healthy dessert and are almost seedless and easily peeled. Satsumas are also one of the most under-estimated fruit trees and could, potentially, be grown in many countries where the climate is unsuitable for most other citrus cultivars.

The Satsuma mandarin is endemic to Japan, where it is known as *unshiu mikan*. It is well adapted to Japan's cold climate and appears to be relatively tolerant to citrus canker (Saunt 1990). The first Satsuma was probably a seedling from a Chinese mandarin, but subsequent bud mutations over hundreds of years have greatly added to the diversity of these plants and they now form a distinct group. One of the problems with this citrus is that bud mutations are so common that it is difficult to ensure that propagated material is true to type.

The Satsuma received its common name in 1878 when General Van Valkenberg, the American ambassador to Japan, imported some plants into the United States; his wife named the trees after Satsuma (now Kagoshima) Prefecture in western Japan. Satsumas have been grown in Japan for several hundred years and many cultivars have been raised, but very few have ever been exported to Europe or America. They are usually treated as a separate species (*Citrus unshiu*), but recent research suggests that are descended from a Chinese mandarin (*C. reticulata*).

Satsumas are the most cold tolerant of all citrus. They have been known to survive temperatures as low as −11°C (12°F) (Webber and Batchelor 1943). They make an excellent first choice for anyone who wishes to grow citrus trees in a cooler climate and will usually produce a small crop of edible fruit. Containerised plants can take a long time to get established, however. Satsumas are extensively grown in Spain, but are less suited to very hot countries, where the fruit may remain green.

Fruit can be left on the tree for decorative effect, but if you want to eat them they should be removed when they are ripe. Older fruit will dry out if they are left on the tree and become rather puffy, the skin breaking away from the internal segments. The fruit subsequently become dry and lose their flavour. Satsumas are harvested in the autumn, but can be stored for a long time if they are kept cool and dry. Most are sold as dessert fruit, but the easily parted segments have made them ideal for canning.

'Aoshima'

'Aoshima' is an excellent Satsuma with large, well-flavoured, almost seedless fruit. The plant was discovered in Japan during 1950 and is currently that country's most popular late-maturing cultivar. The only down side is that 'Aoshima' is an alternate bearer, producing large amounts of fruit in one year and less in the following one. It forms an attractive, vigorous tree with weeping branches and dark green foliage. shoots can reach over 100 centimetres (40 in.) in a single year and should be pruned back by one third to maintain the shape of the tree. The fruit are large, approximately 7 centimetres (2¾ in.) in diameter and approximately 20 percent bigger than those of 'Owari' Satsuma. The majority of the fruit are held at the bottom of the tree.

'Clausellina'

Early ripening has made 'Clausellina' one of the most popular Satsuma cultivars in Spain. The fruit ripens at least two weeks earlier than on the better known 'Owari', from which it arose as a bud mutation in 1962. On

◁ 'Aoshima', one of several Satsuma cultivars in Japan, is rarely seen outside that country.

▷ 'Aoshima' fruit is large and has a sweet flavour.

the down side, the tree is less vigorous than its parent, the fruit is smaller, and the flesh is less sweet and tends to have less flavour. Young trees produce so many fruit in the spring that they have to be thinned to prevent damage to the plant. 'Clausellina' is treated as a dwarf tree when grown on trifoliate orange rootstock.

'Miyagawa'

'Miyagawa' is currently the most popular Satsuma cultivar in Japan, where it is known as *miyagawa wase*. The fruit are larger than those of 'Owari', mature three weeks earlier, and are not as sweet but have a pleasant, if tart, flavour.

'Owari'

'Owari' is by far the most widespread Satsuma cultivar and has a distinctive, weeping habit. The fruit take some time to develop their characteristic colour, but can be eaten when they are still partially green. The plant is very productive and makes an excellent choice for a cool greenhouse. The orange to yellow-orange fruit are oblate (that is, flattened like a pumpkin) or spherical and have conspicuous oil glands on the surface of the skin. They are very juicy, with easily separated segments, and have a delicate, refreshing flavour, with little sign of acidity. The fruit are usually seedless, but may produce a few seeds if they are cross-pollinated. 'Owari' fruit are harvested from November to January in the Northern Hemisphere. The fruit will become puffy and lose most of their flavour if they are left on the tree for too long.

‘Owari’ is the most widely grown Satsuma cultivar and makes an excellent tree for a conservatory. Satsumas need lower temperatures than either oranges or mandarins.

‘Owari’ fruit is very juicy, with easily separated segments and has a delicate, refreshing flavour, with little sign of acidity.

Other Mandarins

‘Changsha’

‘Changsha’ (synonym ‘Ch’ang-sha’) mandarin is one of the hardiest citrus and will withstand temperatures as low as −7.8°C (18°F) (Rieger et al. 2003). It is often listed as a mandarin, but some people believe that it is a hybrid between mandarin (*Citrus reticulata*) and Ichang papeda (*C. ichangensis*). The fruit are deep orange and edible, but have plenty of seeds. This mandarin is named after Changsha, a city in south central China, and comes true from seed.

‘Temple’

‘Temple’ orange, or royal mandarin, was discovered growing wild in

▶ 'Temple' orange is a hybrid between a mandarin and a sweet orange. Because it is easily damaged by frost, the tree is only suitable for a hot climate.

Jamaica in 1896. It is generally believed to be a natural hybrid between sweet orange (*Citrus sinensis*) and mandarin (*C. reticulata*) and was named after William Chace Temple. The deep reddish-orange fruit are round, approximately 7.5 centimetres (3 in.) in diameter, and have a distinctive fragrance. The tree has been extensively planted in Florida, but has a low tolerance to cold and the fruit tend to have many seeds. The fruit, which mature late in the season, are harvested between January and February.

Citrangequats

Citrangequats are trigeneric hybrids, produced by crossing a citrange (*Poncirus trifoliata* × *Citrus sinensis*) with a kumquat (*Fortunella* sp.). Walter Swingle produced the first citrangequats in 1909. 'Thomasville' has sweet, oval or globose, yellow-orange fruit and is considered very hardy. Other cultivars include 'Sinton', 'Telfair', and 'Mr Johns Longevity', most of which are quite thorny.

Grapefruit (Citrus paradisi)

Young grapefruit flowers appear to hang in bunches before they open, which may explain the origin of their name. The fruit are, on the whole, extremely good for you, and half a grapefruit will provide 50 percent of the recommended daily dose of vitamin C. But, grapefruit also contain a chemical that may interfere with the absorption of several prescription drugs by the human digestive system. This includes drugs that are used to control hypertension (blood pressure), statins for the control of high cholesterol, immunosuppressants, anti-histamines, and protease inhibitors.

Grapefruit are only really suited to a hot climate and rarely produce ripe fruit in cooler countries. Most grapefruit are ready for harvesting from March to August in California.

While blood oranges are coloured by anthocyanins, the red pigmentation in pink or red grapefruit is caused by the chemicals beta-carotene and lycopene. Lycopene is a powerful anti-oxidant and has been shown to cause a reduction in cardiovascular disease and prostate cancer. Yellow

◀ Grapefruit trees can reach up to 10 metres (33 ft.) high and need plenty of space to grow properly. They also need a hot climate.

▼ 'Flame' is a slightly pigmented, seedless grapefruit.

◀ There are two types of grapefruit. 'Marsh' is an example of a white grapefruit, while the pigmented cultivars include the dark red 'Star Ruby' and the paler 'Thompson'. Pummelos, by contrast, have a very thick rind (the fruit in the middle).

grapefruit are sometimes called pallid or white-fleshed to distinguish them from their pink relatives, but they still contain low levels of these pigments. The red colour is dependent upon high temperatures, rather than the cool temperatures that are required for colour development in blood oranges.

▷ 'Duncan' grapefruit was first cultivated in the early 1830s, but is still widely grown for its juice.

'Duncan'

'Duncan' is the granddad of all existing grapefruit cultivars. All other grapefruit can trace their ancestry to this plant. The original specimen grew on the Pinellas Peninsula in Florida and was nearly one hundred years old when it died. A second plant of the same parentage grew nearby and was the source of all the material that was subsequently propagated. According to Webber and Batchelor (1943), this second tree eventually grew to a height of 14 metres (45 ft.) and had a girth of almost 2.4 metres (8 ft.) in 1932. The plant remained unnamed for many years, but was eventually propagated by A. L. Duncan in 1892 and given his name.

'Duncan' grapefruit have an excellent flavour. Although they have many seeds, they are still grown extensively in Florida for juice. The fruit are light yellow with a smooth surface.

'Marsh'

Pop into your local supermarket to buy a grapefruit and it will almost certainly be a 'Marsh' (synonyms 'Marsh Seedless', 'White Marsh', 'Whitney'). The flesh is pale yellow, very juicy, and has a good flavour. 'Marsh' was the first seedless grapefruit and became an immediate commercial success. It still dominates the commercial market and the bulk of all grapefruit juice is still obtained from this cultivar. All pigmented grapefruit are descended from this grapefruit. The original plant was a chance seedling from a 'Duncan'

"Marsh' is the world's most popular grapefruit. The tree produces large amounts of fruit, but needs warm conditions.

grapefruit in 1860 and was named by C. M. Marsh, who acquired the orchard in 1892. The trees are very vigorous, but will only produce a commercial crop in a very hot climate. The fruit are a similar shape and colour to 'Duncan' fruit, but have a thicker peel. They are harvested from November to May in Florida.

'Hudson'

'Hudson' grapefruit appeared as a bud mutation of 'Foster' pink grapefruit in the 1950s, but while it had deeper pink flesh than its parent, the fruit were very seedy. To counter this, breeders irradiated the seed and produced 'Star Ruby', an almost seedless cultivar, with deep red flesh. 'Hudson' was a commercial failure because of the large number of seeds.

'Rio Red'

'Rio Red' grapefruit was produced from the irradiated budwood of 'Ruby' grapefruit and introduced in 1984. The flesh is burgundy-red, almost as dark as 'Star Ruby', and about three times darker than that of 'Ruby'. 'Rio Red' grows to form a large tree and is claimed to be less finicky about its growing conditions than 'Star Ruby'. The fruit often have a pink-flushed skin, particularly if two or more fruit are growing together, and measure up to 9 centimetres (3½ in.) across. They can be harvested from November to March.

'Ruby'

For many years 'Ruby' (synonyms 'Redblush', 'Ruby Red') was the darkest of all pigmented grapefruit, but it has lost that distinction to 'Star Ruby', which has considerably deeper pigmented flesh. Young fruit are yellow, like a white-fleshed cultivar, and need plenty of heat before they develop any external blush. 'Ruby' originated as a bud mutation on 'Thompson' grapefruit in 1926.

'Star Ruby'

'Star Ruby' (synonyms 'Jaffa Sunrise', 'Sunrise') was first introduced onto the commercial market in 1970, but it has taken a long time for this grapefruit to become widely available in European supermarkets. The young fruit are apricot-coloured and flushed with red pigment, maturing to a deep pinkish orange. The flesh is deep pinkish red, with few, if any seeds and produces sweeter juice than 'Ruby' grapefruit. The fruit can be difficult to peel and have dark oil glands on the surface of the skin. The skin of organic fruit has a particularly intense fragrance.

'Star Ruby' was created in 1959 by irradiating seed from 'Hudson' grapefruit. While the parent had deeper red flesh, it also had many seeds. 'Star Ruby' is an attractive plant, but is less vigorous than most other grapefruit and rather sensitive to sunburn and herbicides. The mature fruit are also slightly smaller than other red cultivars, but have the deepest red colouration. They need plenty of heat, but the internal colour will eventually develop in cooler climates if the fruit are left on the tree.

▶ 'Star Ruby' has the most deeply pigmented flesh of any grapefruit. The fruit have become very popular, but the trees are less vigorous than the older established varieties.

'Thompson'

'Thompson' (synonym 'Pink Marsh') arose as a bud mutation on 'Marsh' grapefruit at some time prior to the First World War. It was the first grapefruit to have pigmented flesh and is often sold as 'Pink Marsh' or simply as a pink grapefruit. The fruit looks almost identical to a typical 'Marsh', but has a slightly darker skin and pale pink flesh. It was named after W. Thompson of Florida, the owner of the orchard where the mutation was found.

Pummelo (*Citrus maxima*)

The pummelo, also known as the shaddock, is native to Southeast Asia and is widely cultivated in southern China, where it was probably introduced in the first century A.D. (Morton 1987). The fruit are highly regarded in Southeast Asia and are the largest of all citrus, occasionally weighing up to 2 kg (about 4 lbs.) each. The trees require plenty of heat and have a rather weeping habit, with the majority of the massive fruit suspended from the bottom of the tree. Mature trees can grow up to 15 metres (50 ft.) high and have trunks that measure up to 30 centimetres (12 in.) thick. The leaves are very large and leathery, and measure up to 12 centimetres (4¾ in.) across and 20 centimetres (8 in.) long. Pummelos are seedless when grown in isolation from other citrus.

Most pummelos are grown from seed, but there are several clonal cultivars in Asia, such as 'Kinokawa' (synonym 'Kinokawa Buntan') from Japan, 'Pomelit' from Indonesia, and 'Kao Pan', 'Kao Yai', and 'Thong Dee' from Thailand.

Mature pummelos look like large grapefruit, but have a very thick mesocarp and slightly fewer segments than their better-known relatives. Some pummelos, such as 'Oroblanco', have a green skin, while others turn yellow or golden yellow as the fruit ages. In Thailand the peel is removed and the segments separated, the flesh is then removed from the membranes and

▲ 'Kinokawa' pummelo is named after a river in Japan.

▶ *Citrus maxima* (pummelo or shaddock) is mainly grown in Southeast Asia, where there are numerous local cultivars. The fruit are the largest in the genus.

eaten separately. The flesh is less sweet than that of grapefruit, but has a pleasant, rather aromatic flavour.

Pummelo trees are so large that they are probably unsuitable for growing in containers and few people would be able to provide sufficient heat for them to produce edible fruit in any case. Pummelos have very good storage properties and can be kept for two to three months without showing any sign of deterioration. Some cultivars are thought to be several hundred years old and, in many cases, are probably infected by viruses such as tristeza.

In the late 1950s scientists at the University of California in Riverside raised two hybrids between a pummelo and a grapefruit, named 'Melogold' and 'Oroblanco', and another hybrid between a sweet pummelo and a pink pummelo, called 'Chandler'. These plants were patented by the University and consequently cannot be propagated without its permission. The skin of these hybrid fruit is thicker than a grapefruit, but thinner than a typical pummelo. The hybrid fruit are produced in clusters and hang among the leaves at the bottom of the tree.

▶ 'Chandler' pummelo has a greenish-yellow rind and deep pink flesh.

'Chandler'

'Chandler' (synonym 'Jaffa Red Pomelo') is an improbable-looking fruit that can weigh up to 1 kilogram (about 2 lbs.). It has sweet, deep pink flesh. The thick, deep greenish yellow skin surrounds a very thick spongy mesocarp.

The plant was bred by J. Cameron and R. Soost at the University of California, Riverside, and is a hybrid between a Siamese pink pummelo and a Siamese sweet pummelo. The fruit tend to be rather seedy if they are grown near other compatible citrus cultivars, but are seedless when grown next to incompatible fruit, such as satsumas. Mature fruit have a diameter of 12.5 centimetres (5 in.), approximately 25 percent bigger than the average grapefruit, and are harvested between January and April in California. 'Chandler' pummelos are incredibly productive, producing as much as 35 tonnes of fruit per hectare (14 tonnes per acre) (Becerra-Rodríguez et al. 2007).

There is a lot of confusion about this hybrid pummelo. On the Internet there are several references to it being the ancestor of the grapefruit, which is not true.

'Cocktail Grapefruit'

Not strictly a grapefruit, 'Cocktail Grapefruit' is a hybrid between 'Frua' mandarin and a Siamese sweet pummelo. It originated at the University of California, Riverside, in the 1950s and somehow found its way into commercial production. The fruit look like white grapefruit but have very sweet, yellowish-orange flesh and plenty of seeds. The fruit are harvested from November to February.

'Melogold'

'Melogold' is a hybrid between a Siamese sweet pummelo and a grapefruit and was released in 1986. It looks like a large grapefruit, but tastes like a pummelo. Young plants have larger fruit, but these reduce in size as the plant matures. Mature fruit have a tendency to fall off the tree, so they are usually harvested when slightly green. The fruit continues to mature until they are golden yellow. A typical fruit measures approximately 10 centimetres (4 in.) across and weighs 500 to 600 grams (around 1 lb.). The fruit can be harvested from December to May in California.

'Oroblanco'

'Oroblanco' (synonyms 'Jaffa Sweetie', 'Sweetie'), a hybrid between a Siamese sweet pummelo and a white grapefruit, produces slightly smaller fruit than its sibling 'Melogold', but they are very sweet and have no hint of the bitterness that is normally present in grapefruit. The fruit are slightly larger than those of a grapefruit and have a yellowish-green skin when they are ripe. The flesh is pale yellow and has a mild flavour. 'Oroblanco' needs lower temperatures than a grapefruit and may be a good choice for home gardeners in cooler countries. Mature fruit measure approximately 9 centimetres (3½ in.) across and weigh between 400 and 500 grams (around 1 lb.). The fruit can be harvested from December to May in California.

'Oroblanco' pummelo, showing fruit hidden in the foliage. Citrus fruit can be damaged by very strong sunshine, which literally cooks the fruit on the tree.

'Oroblanco' looks very much like a grapefruit, but has a thicker rind. The fruit are very sweet and mature earlier than a grapefruit.

Ugli®

The old adage 'Never judge a book by its cover' certainly applies to this citrus fruit. The skin may be wrinkly and green, but the interior is sweet and juicy. I don't know who chose the name, but it intrigues children.

The plant was found growing wild in Jamaica in 1914 and is thought to be a cross between a tangerine and a pummelo—a tangelo. Cabel Hall Citrus, the owner of the registered name, says that it is a hybrid between a Seville orange, a grapefruit, and a tangerine.

The very large fruit have a thick rind, which is deeply wrinkled on the surface. They need very high temperatures to achieve the necessary sweetness

Ugli® tangelo is grown commercially only in Jamaica, where there is sufficient heat for the fruit to mature. Pictured here is a young tree.

and rarely perform well in countries with a subtropical climate. The fruit are mature even though the rind is partially green, but sell better when they have developed their typical deep yellow-orange colour. They can be harvested from late December, but attain their best flavour in the spring. The fruit are exported by the Jamaican company Trout Hall, the sole export-license holder.

◀ Ugli® tangelo, a cross between a pummelo and a mandarin, is aptly named for its very wrinkled fruit.

▼ Ugli® fruit are mature even though the rind is partially green.

◀ 'Wheeny' pummelo has juicy yellow flesh and needs less heat to grow than do true grapefruit.

'Wheeny'
'Wheeny' pummelo is actually a hybrid between a true grapefruit and a pummelo and was named after Wheeny Creek in Australia, where it was raised in the 1930s. It has juicy, pale yellow flesh but is prone to alternate

cropping. The plant needs lower temperatures than true grapefruit and is grown successfully in New Zealand.

Lemons (Citrus limon)

Lemon trees are extremely vigorous and need regular pruning to keep them in shape. Two cultivars dominate the commercial market: 'Garey's Eureka' and 'Lisbon'. Spain also produces large quantities of 'Verna', which accounts for 70 percent of its lemon crop. Many countries also have their own lemon cultivars, which were raised locally and are usually well adapted to the local climate.

Most lemons can be harvested throughout the year. Lemon trees do not become dormant in the winter and tend to produce some flowers throughout the year. However, this makes them more vulnerable to cold weather than oranges and they will usually shed their foliage if the temperature drops below −5°C (23°F). Fruit are badly damaged by temperatures below −2°C (28°F) and serious damage can occur to the wood when temperatures fall below −7°C (19°F) (Morton 1987). 'Improved Meyer' is slightly hardier than true lemon and may be a better choice for home gardeners in a cold climate.

'Femminello'
'Femminello' (synonyms 'Femminello Commune', 'Femminello Ovale') is the most widely cultivated lemon in Italy, where there are several named selections. The trees flower throughout the year in Italy and each season's crop is given a different name. The first crop is collected from winter to spring and is called the Limoni. The Bianchetti crop is collected from spring to early summer, and the Verdelli during the hot summer months from June to September. The final crop, the Primofiori, is harvested in autumn. Each crop has its own characteristics and is the result of slightly different growing conditions.

The fruit of 'Femminello' differ in shape from the more ubiquitous 'Garey's Eureka' and 'Lisbon' lemons, with a shorter nipple and a short or long neck. Mature fruit have a yellow skin and greenish-yellow flesh with very few seeds. This cultivar is vulnerable to mal secco disease.

'Garey's Eureka'
This extremely popular lemon started life as a pip in a batch of Sicilian lemons. The seeds were planted in Los Angeles, California, and produced

several hundred seedlings. In 1860 a number of the seedlings were sold to Andrew Ball, whose son-in-law gave budwood from one of them to Thomas Garey, a Los Angeles nurseryman. The correct name is 'Garey's Eureka', but this cultivar is usually referred to simply as 'Eureka' lemon.

Mature fruit are bright yellow and have a pleasant fragrance. They are elliptical to obovate, with a short neck and a conspicuous nipple. 'Eureka' trees are smaller than 'Lisbon' trees, have less foliage, and are less cold hardy, but they start producing fruit at an earlier age and continue bearing fruit over a longer period of time. Young plants of 'Eureka' may produce so many fruit that they can damage the tree. Excess fruit should be removed with a pair of secateurs.

'Lisbon'

'Lisbon' is a very vigorous lemon cultivar and, given time, will grow to form a large tree with upright branches and dense foliage. It originated in Australia and was probably grown from seed that originated in Portugal. American growers imported a number of trees into California between 1874 and 1875 and the cultivar has subsequently become widespread in both that state and Arizona. Several clones of 'Lisbon' exist today, suggesting that the original trees were seedlings from a common parent. These clones differ in subtle ways, such as their vigour, amount of foliage, quality of fruit, and size of thorns.

▲ 'Frost Lisbon' lemon is a selection of 'Lisbon'.

▶ 'Lisbon' lemon is hardier than 'Eureka', but has rather thorny bushes.

'Lisbon' lemon can be grown on a trifoliate orange rootstock, while its main competitor ('Eureka') cannot. 'Lisbon' trees are more productive than 'Eureka' trees, and the fruit tends to be hidden among the branches, where it is protected from sun scorch and cold, but increases the risk of injury to fruit pickers when the fruit are being harvested. 'Lisbon' is more cold resistant than 'Eureka' and is widely grown in Australia, California, Uruguay, and Argentina. The lemon-yellow fruit are elliptical or oblong, with a pronounced nipple at the stylar end and a short neck. 'Frost Lisbon' is a selection of 'Lisbon' named after the geneticist, who raised it.

'Meyer' (*Citrus* ×*meyeri*)

'Meyer' lemons are an excellent substitute for true lemons if you live in a cold country. They make good pot plants and produce tasty fruit throughout the year. They are very useful if you are cooking and haven't got enough time to pop down to the local supermarket and grab a bag of real lemons.

Although 'Meyer' is usually listed among lemons, it is actually a hybrid between a lemon and a mandarin or an orange. It was first found growing as a pot plant near Beijing, China, in 1908, by Frank Meyer, a plant collector for the U.S. Department of Agriculture. The foliage looks similar to that of a lemon, but the fruit is more rounded, with a smooth, rather thin, light orange-yellow skin. The distinctive nipples at either end of true lemon fruit are small and inconspicuous in 'Meyer' lemon.

◀ 'Meyer' lemon fruit are round rather than being spindle-shaped and the trees tolerate lower temperatures than true lemons. Because this cultivar harbours citrus tristeza disease, readers should only purchase 'Improved Meyer', which is free of the disease.

The original 'Meyer' lemon was popular as a backyard citrus plant because it could be grown from cuttings, but in the 1940s it was discovered that it was a symptomless carrier of citrus tristeza virus (CTV). Commercial citrus growers were told to destroy their plants. In the 1950s, California-based Four Winds Growers discovered a virus-free clone. This new plant was certified as being virus-free by the University of California and released to the market as 'Improved Meyer' in the 1970s. Readers should only buy 'Improved Meyer' and should avoid propagating older plants that could still be harbouring CTV. The sale of the original, un-improved 'Meyer' lemon is prohibited in California.

'Meyer' tolerates much lower temperatures than a true lemon, but has little value as a commercial crop. The fruit are easily damaged during transport and the peel yields little oil. 'Meyer' is a semi-dwarf, thornless tree and makes a good choice for the home gardener.

'Variegated Eureka'

This decorative lemon can often be found for sale in European garden centres, but actually originates from the United States. The foliage is variegated and, when young, the fruit are covered with green and cream stripes. Mature fruit are yellow with pink oil glands and pale pink flesh. The young flower buds and shoots are fuchsia-pink in colour. 'Variegated Eureka' is grown as an ornamental plant and has no commercial value. It arose as a sport of 'Garey's Eureka'.

'Verna'

'Verna' is mainly grown in Spain, where it originated, but is also cultivated to a lesser extent in Morocco and Algeria. Mature trees are quite large with very few thorns and usually produce two, or occasionally three, crops of fruit per year. 'Verna' is widely grown because it bears fruit when other varieties of lemon are unavailable. The main crop is produced from spring flowers, but the tree also flowers in the summer and produces a second crop of fruit called the Verdi. Lemons of the main crop are rather elongated with a pronounced nipple at the stylar end and an extended neck, while the Verdi are more rounded and have a thinner skin. 'Verna' fruit are almost seedless, with a thick, pale yellow skin. This cultivar is usually grafted onto a sour orange rootstock and, increasingly, on the citrange 'Troyer'.

'Villafranca'

This lemon originated in Sicily and was formerly widely cultivated in Florida. The trees are quite thorny and not very productive. The fruit is rather seedy. Most fruit appears in the summer, but apart from that difference, mature trees and fruit look almost identical to those of 'Garey's Eureka'. 'Villafranca' has never been widely planted in California, but is popular in Israel.

Citrus pyriformis 'Ponderosa'

Otherwise known as 'American Wonder' lemon, this small tree produces large, orange-yellow fruit with rather sour-tasting, pale greenish-yellow flesh. Its true parentage is a mystery, but it is probably a hybrid between a citron and a lemon. The fruit is of low quality, so the tree is usually grown as an ornamental plant. It makes an especially good espalier tree. 'Ponderosa' has stout, rather spiny branches and large elliptical leaves with a crenulated margin.

▲ *Citrus pyriformis* (lemon) 'Ponderosa' is a popular garden plant in hotter parts of the United States. The tree has very spiny stems, but produces very sweet fruit.

Citrus lumia

Citrus lumia (synonym *C. limon* var. *lumia*) is a tall-growing lemon with very large, elliptic leaves and massive, pale yellow fruit. The pear-shaped fruit have a pronounced nipple at the stylar end and hang on the tree in groups of three to ten.

'Bitrouni'

Citrus lumia was crossed with a lemon to produce 'Bitrouni'. The large, deep yellow fruit have a rather knobbly skin.

▷ 'Bitrouni' lemon produces large, bright yellow fruit.

'Pear Lemon'
'Adam's Apple'

'Pear Lemon' and 'Adam's Apple' have been known for hundred of years, but they don't fit happily into any of the existing classification systems. Risso and Poiteau (1818–1822) included both of them in *Citrus lumia*, while Swingle (1943) placed 'Pear Lemon' with the lemons (*C. limon* var. *lumia*) and Webber and Batchelor (1943) allocated 'Adam's Apple' to the citrons. Both are usually listed as citron cultivars; however, a group of Italian scientists has now shown that the two cultivars have the same ancestry and are probably the result of a cross between a citron and a pummelo, with the offspring then being crossed with a lemon (Nicolosi et al. 2000). 'Adam's Apple' was first recorded in the Holy Land in the thirteenth century (Gallesio 1811), so the initial hybridisation presumably occurred at an earlier date in an area where all three species (*C. medica*, *C. maxima*, and *C. limon*) were growing, presumably in Indochina.

Fruit of the aptly named 'Pear Lemon' (synonyms 'Pero del Commendatore', 'Poir du Commandeur') measures up to 20 centimetres (8 in.) long and has a long tapering neck. The skin is yellow and very thick. An illustration of the fruit was published in Risso and Poiteau's *Histoire naturelle des orangers* (1818–1822, plate 67).

'Adam's Apple' (synonyms 'Pomme d'Adam', 'Pomme du Paradis') has been cultivated in Europe for several hundred years, but has no commercial use and is rarely seen now. It is illustrated as *Limonium pomum Adami* in Risso and Poiteau's *Histoire naturelle des orangers* (1818–1822, plate 60).

Limes

Limes appear to be very confusing, but in practice only three species are likely to be found. The situation is not helped by the fact that one species (*Citrus aurantifolia*) is known by three different names: West Indian lime, Mexican lime, and Key lime.

Limes are usually harvested before they are ripe, because consumers expect them to be green in colour. Mature limes are actually coloured yellow-green or yellow. The fruit of the West Indian lime are more aromatic and said to have a better flavour than those of 'Tahiti' and 'Bearss'. Lime trees can be distinguished from lemons when they are not in fruit by the wide petioles.

If you want to grow a lime in a container, I would always recommend 'Tahiti'. The West Indian lime tree has vicious thorns and needs much higher temperatures than 'Tahiti'.

'Tahiti' (*Citrus latifolia*)

'Tahiti' (synonyms 'Page', 'Persian') is the best lime for a cool climate. It still needs plenty of heat, but will bear fruit throughout the year and is always on call if you need a slice of lime for your glass of vodka or gin.

This lime has a very long, but rather obscure history. The plant probably originated in Southeast Asia and found its way to Europe, via Persia (now Iran). It acquired its name because the first plants to reach the United States originated from the island of Tahiti in the Pacific Ocean.

The trees are bigger than those of the West Indian lime (Citrus aurantifolia) and have larger leaves and very few thorns. The fruit are deep green when young, but turn yellow-green and then yellow as they become fully ripe; they are larger than the fruit of West Indian lime, are oval, and have a very thin skin. Mature trees grow to a height of 3–5 metres (10–16 ft.) and eventually develop a substantial trunk. The elliptic leaves have short petioles and a crenate margin.

'Tahiti' can be grafted onto a wide range of rootstocks, but grafts on 'Cleopatra' mandarin and Rangpur lime tend to be short-lived (Stenzel and Neves 2004). The fruit is harvested from July to December in California.

▶ 'Tahiti' (*Citrus latifolia*) lime is much hardier than Mexican lime (*C. aurantifolia*).

'Bearss' (*Citrus latifolia*)

There is a lot of confusion about 'Bearss' (the correct spelling is 'Bearss' as opposed to 'Bears'), because some people consider it to be identical to 'Tahiti' lime. The plant probably originated as a seedling from a 'Tahiti' lime and was named by T. J. Bears, who found it growing in his Californian nursery around 1895. The trees are more erect and larger than those of 'Tahiti' lime and produce larger, almost seedless fruit. The fruit are harvested from September to December in California.

West Indian lime (*Citrus aurantifolia*)

Citrus aurantifolia is thought to have originated in Malaysia, but is now cultivated in many hot countries throughout the world. As far as we know, the plant was obtained by Arab traders, who took it to the Middle East and North Africa. It was cultivated in Italy during the Middle Ages after being introduced into Europe by the Crusaders. The Spanish subsequently took it to their colonies in the West Indies and South America. *Citrus aurantifolia* is known as Key lime in Florida and as West Indian lime in California. (Note that both names are used as common names as well as cultivar names, adding to the nomenclatural confusion.) This citrus is also known as Mexican lime and bartender's lime.

Mature West Indian lime trees are slightly smaller than 'Tahiti' lime trees and grow to a height of 2–4 metres (6–13 ft.). They are very drought tolerant, but have numerous small thorns. The fruit are round to oval with a small nipple, a strong flavour, and many small seeds. West Indian lime needs considerably higher temperatures than 'Tahiti' or 'Bearss'.

Most West Indian lime trees are propagated from seed and show considerable variability, both in habit and productivity. Plants for commercial nurseries are increasingly propagated from selected material and grafted onto sour orange (*Citrus aurantium*), rough lemon (*C. jambhiri*), or trifoliate orange (*Poncirus trifoliata*) rootstocks. Commercial production is concentrated in Mexico, Egypt, and the West Indies. West Indian lime is rarely grown in the United States.

Rangpur (*Citrus limonia*)

Citrus limonia is usually included with limes because of its highly acidic and bitter juice, but it is probably a hybrid between a mandarin and a rough lemon (*Citrus jambhiri*).

Rangpur produces a vigorous tree with thorny twigs. It grows to between 5 and 7 metres (16–23 ft.) high. Mature plants produce large numbers of small reddish-orange fruit with very bitter juice. This fruit is sometimes used as a substitute for true limes.

Rangpur is occasionally used as a rootstock, in which cases it imparts a particularly high tolerance to salt. The tree tolerates drought and calcareous soil, but is prone to phytophthora and citrus scab. Grafted plants have a tendency to die back after a few years.

'Makrut' (*Citrus hystrix*)

'Makrut' lime, also known as Thai lime, is a wonderful plant, with many uses, but don't try to eat the fruit. I can guarantee that you won't forget the experience. *Citrus hystrix* is the only member of the genus where the foliage is harvested as a crop, rather than the fruit. The plant is widely grown in Thailand and imparts a characteristic flavour to a range of Thai dishes, including soup and curries. An extract from the fruit is used as a hair shampoo, a bleaching agent during washing, and a natural air freshener. The glossy, dark green leaves have a distinctive shape, with very broad petioles (illustrated on page 39). Mature fruit are yellow and have numerous seeds, but they are usually harvested when they are still green. They produce very little juice and have a distinctive, knobbly exterior.

This lime is quite easy to grow, but needs plenty of heat and sunshine. It forms a small, bushy tree, with rather thin branches and glossy, dark green leaves. The petioles are almost as large as the true leaves and give the plants a distinctive appearance. The branches are covered with sharp thorns, but these are rarely a problem if you are careful.

'Makrut' lime is known as limau purut in Malaysia, bai makrut in Thailand, and daun jerak in Indonesia. It has also been called 'Kaffir' lime, from the Arabic word kafir, meaning non-believer or infidel, but in some countries and cultures, such as South Africa, that word is highly offensive.

▶ 'Makrut' lime has distinctive, but inedible, bumpy fruit, which are dark green when young and turn yellow as they mature.

The leaves of *Citrus ichangensis* (Ichang papeda or Yichang orange) look very similar to those of *C. hystrix* and have broad petioles. This species is the hardiest member of the genus *Citrus* and can be grown outside in cool temperate parts of the United States and northern Europe. The fruit are inedible, but are used to perfume rooms in China. The plant forms a small shrub, with sharp spines.

Citrons (Citrus medica)

Citron grows naturally in the foothills of the Himalaya mountain range and has been known in Europe since at least 310 B.C., when Theophrastus referred to it as the Median or Persian apple. Citron pips were also found during excavations in ancient Mesopotamia, which suggests that the fruit, if not the plants themselves, have been appreciated for a long time (Killerman 1916). The Latin species name does not refer to any medical uses of the plant, but to the fact that citrons were first cultivated by the Medes, who lived in an area that is now included in Iran.

Citrus medica var. sarcodactylis

Citrus medica var. *sarcodactylis* (synonym *C. medica* var. *digitata*) is known as 'Buddha's Hand' citron, fingered citron, and *cidro digitado*. It is one of the oddest fruit in existence and always attracts attention. The plant looks similar to a normal citron, but the fruit have numerous fingerlike projections and very little pulp. The tree isn't very vigorous and seems to take a long time to become established, but it is worth persisting. It also needs plenty of heat. Mature trees form a rather low bush, with many spreading branches. The fruit turn deep yellow-orange when they are ripe and have a wonderful fragrance, but they need plenty of heat to develop properly. In Japan and China the fruit are used to perfume clothing. They have an incredible scent that quickly permeates an entire room.

◀ *Citrus medica* var. *sarcodactylis* is highly valued in the Far East, where the fruit are used to perfume laundry.

'Etrog'

'Etrog' is a small, spindle-shaped citron used in the Jewish Feast of Tabernacles. Plants must be grown on their own roots if they are to be considered kosher and must not be grafted. 'Etrog' may be the original, wild form of the species, from which the larger cultivated forms have been subsequently derived. It is repeat flowering.

'Aurantiata'

'Aurantiata' (synonyms Chinese citron, orange citron) has a similar shape to the normal cultivar but is orange-yellow with a very warty skin.

Kumquats (Fortunella spp.)

The genus *Fortunella* includes three species that are grown for their fruit, namely, *F. margarita* ('Nagami' kumquat), *F. japonica* ('Marumi' kumquat), and *F. crassifolia* ('Meiwa' kumquat). A fourth species, *F. hindsii*, has tiny, pea-sized fruit and is grown solely as an ornamental plant. The genus is named after Robert Fortune, the famous plant collector, who found *F. margarita* growing in China; the species is presumed to be native to the southern part of that country.

Kumquats are prone to a zinc deficiency, which results in smaller leaves and shorter shoots. They have always been considered very hardy, although this may be largely due to their long winter dormancy. Their cold tolerance has led to them being crossed with a number of other citrus species, such as limes, which usually need high temperatures to produce edible fruit. The offspring are usually much hardier than the citrus parent, but tend to have smaller fruit. The hybrids are denoted by the suffix '-*quat*' (for example, limequat, orangequat). Kumquats can be harvested from November to April in California.

'Nagami' (*Fortunella margarita*)

'Nagami', also known as oval kumquat, is a small tree with lanceolate leaves and slightly spiny branches. A potted plant will normally grow to a height of approximately 1.25 metres (4 ft.), but outdoors will usually reach 4 metres (13 ft.) tall or more. It produces masses of small, bright orange oval fruit, which are sold as a

▶ 'Nagami' kumquat forms an attractive, quite hardy tree that becomes semi-dormant in the winter.

'Nagami' produces lanceolate leaves and masses of small fruit on slightly spiny branches.

'Nagami' is the most commonly grown kumquat. Its deep orange, oval fruit are often sold as a delicacy and can be preserved as candy.

delicacy in Western supermarkets. In warm countries *Fortunella margarita* will eventually grow to form a substantial, very ornamental tree. The fruit are harvested from October to January and can be candied.

'Marumi' (*Fortunella japonica*)

'Marumi', also called round kumquat, is less popular than oval kumquat, partly due to its thornier branches and smaller fruit. The fruit are slightly sweeter than the oval kumquat and have fewer seeds.

'Meiwa' (*Fortunella crassifolia*)

'Meiwa' kumquat is probably a natural hybrid between *Fortunella margarita* and *F. japonica*. It is grown in China and Japan, but rarely seen else-

'Meiwa' fruit are the size of a small tomato.

'Meiwa' kumquat is rarely found outside Japan and China. A hybrid between *Fortunella margarita* and *F. japonica*, it has larger, sweeter fruit than either of its parents.

where. It is more cold resistant than either of the parents and has larger, sweeter fruit, which measure approximately 25 mm (1 in.) across. Trifoliate orange (*Poncirus trifoliata*) is considered to be the best rootstock.

'Calamondin' (×*Citrofortunella microcarpa*)

'Calamondin' (synonym 'Four Seasons') is probably a hybrid between mandarin (*Citrus reticulata*) and kumquat (*Fortunella* sp.), but is traditionally listed with kumquats. The plant probably originated in the Philippines and then spread to China and Indonesia. From there it reached India, the remainder of South Asia, the West Indies, and eventually the United States, where it thrives outdoors in Florida and Texas, but may be damaged by frost in parts of California.

'Calamondin' is one of the few citrus trees that can be grown successfully indoors and is widely sold as a houseplant. Mature specimens will often grow to a height of 6 metres (20 ft.) in a hot climate, but potted plants rarely exceed 1 metre (3 ft.). The plant forms an attractive, upright tree with winged petioles and the occasional thorn. It produces masses of flowers and later in the year a crop of small, sweet fruit, measuring between 2.5 and 4 centimetres (1–1½ in.) across. The fruit have a number of small seeds. The tree tolerates relatively low light levels, but benefits from being sprayed regularly with lukewarm rainwater, which keeps it healthy and reduces the incidence of black mould and red spider mite. The plants can become infested with aphids, but be very careful what you spray them with if you intend to eat the fruit.

This cultivar is often sold as a miniature bonsai tree in Europe. The seedlings can be used as rootstocks for kumquats. The variegated form of

▼ 'Calamondin' is probably a hybrid between a kumquat (*Fortunella* sp.) and a mandarin (*Citrus reticulata*). The fruit have several culinary uses.

◀ 'Calamondin' kumquat can grow to a height of 6 metres (20 ft.) in a Mediterranean climate, but is one of the few citrus trees that can be grown as a true houseplant.

'Calamondin' orange has green- and yellow-striped young fruit, and variegated foliage.

Limequats (×*Citrofortunella*)

These attractive trees are hybrids between lime (*Citrus aurantifolia*) and kumquat (*Fortunella* sp.). The resulting hybrid has fruits like a lime, but will tolerate significantly lower temperatures. There are three cultivars, all raised in 1909 by Walter Swingle, while he was working for the U.S. Department of Agriculture in Eustis, Florida. The fruit typically have a lot of seeds.

Limequats form an open, thorny bush with strong, arching stems. The fruit smell like limes when they are squeezed and have a pleasant after-scent.

◁ Limequats form small, neat trees with spreading branches. They are quite thorny.

▷ Limequats are hybrids between lime (*Citrus aurantifolia*) and kumquat (*Fortunella* sp.) with fruits like a lime.

'Eustis'

Walter Swingle produced 'Eustis' in 1909, by crossing West Indian lime (*Citrus aurantifolia*) with 'Marumi' kumquat (*Fortunella japonica*). The resulting plant forms a small tree with spreading branches. The roughly oval or round fruit are similar in size to kumquat fruit at approximately 3 × 4 cm (1¼ × 1½ in.), with the flavour of a lime. The rind is pale yellow

> 'Eustis' limequat has small lime-flavoured fruit with a sweet-tasting rind.

with a green tinge and surprisingly sweet to the taste. 'Eustis' needs a minimum temperature of 10°C (50°F).

'Lakeland'

'Lakeland' limquat came from the same cross as 'Eustis' but has much larger oval fruit, measuring approximately 4.5 × 7 centimetres (1¾ × 2¾ in.). The fruit are yellow and have a taste similar to Mexican lime (*Citrus aurantifolia*). 'Lakeland' was named after a city in Florida.

'Tavares'

The fruit of 'Tavares' look similar to 'Eustis' fruit, but 'Tavares' flower buds are pink whereas those of 'Eustis' are white. The oval, orange-yellow fruit measure approximately 3 × 5 centimetres (1¼ × 2 in.). The cultivar was named after Tavares, a town in Florida, and was bred by crossing Mexican lime (*Citrus aurantifolia*) with oval kumquat (*Fortunella margarita*).

◀ 'Tavares' has small oval orange-yellow fruit.

▶ 'Tavares' limequat, named after a town in Florida, forms an attractive tree.

Sour Orange (Citrus aurantium)

Sour orange, or bigarade, has been cultivated in Europe since the early Middle Ages. Several unusual mutations have occurred during this time and many are illustrated in Risso and Poiteau's *Histoire naturelle des orangers* (1818–1822). In this group are cultivars with knobbly fruit and variegated leaves. Many of these have probably been lost to cultivation, but several (such as 'Bizzaria' and 'Fasciata') have survived in old collections. They are difficult to obtain, but are likely to become more readily available as interest in citrus trees grows.

Sour orange (*Citrus aurantium*) trees usually can be distinguished from sweet orange (*C. sinensis*) trees by the absence of a grafting scar on the trunk and the longer, more broadly winged petioles. Sour orange is tolerant of phytophthora and can be grown on its own roots, without any need for grafting; however, because it is very vulnerable to citrus tristeza virus, it is rarely used as a rootstock today. The petioles of a mature

◁ A mature sour orange tree growing on the Spanish island of Majorca.

▽ Seville sour orange trees line the streets of Inca on the island of Majorca.

▽ Orange trees are used for decoration in the town of Sóller in North Majorca.

sour orange tree are almost twice the length of those of a sweet orange, while the oil glands on the sour orange fruit are slightly concave (sunken), as opposed to being convex (raised) in the sweet orange.

Sour oranges tolerate much colder weather than sweet oranges and were one of the first plants to be used as a rootstock for other citrus. They are widely grown along the streets of Mediterranean towns and cities and form attractive, small to medium-sized trees with dark green, evergreen foliage. The fruit are usually harvested in January.

Citrus aurantium var. *myrtifolia*, commonly known as myrtle-leaved orange, is very popular in Italy, where it is known as *chinotto*, after China, its place of origin. Sometimes treated as a separate species (*Citrus myrtifolia*), myrtle-leaved orange has small elliptical leaves like true myrtle (*Myrtus communis*) and bears masses of small orange fruit. The fruit are very bitter, but they can be candied and are used to make a commercial soft drink. Four cultivars are known: 'Chinotto Grande' (large chinotto), 'Chinotto Piccolo' (small chinotto), 'Chinotto Crispifolia' (crisped-leaved chinotto), and 'Chinotto Buxifolia' (box-leaved chinotto).

Citrus aurantium var. *salicifolia*, or willow-leaved orange, has dark green, elliptical leaves like those of a willow tree. *Citrus aurantium* var. *caniculata* is an interesting form of sour orange, with distinctive fluted fruit.

Several commercial cultivars of sour orange are known, but Seville (the name is sometimes used as a common name) is by far the most popular. Its round, deep orange fruit have a rather thick skin with a rough surface. Seville oranges look very tempting, but the flesh is extremely bitter and cannot be eaten as dessert fruit. Still, sour oranges grow well in containers and are hardier than sweet oranges.

Sour oranges make a good choice for the indoor gardener. The plants have the same appearance as the sweet orange, but are much hardier and will remain healthy in cool situations.

'Bizzaria'

This unusual plant was first described by Pietro Nati as *La Bizzaria* in 1674 and was illustrated as bigaradier bizzarrerie in Risso and Poiteau's *Histoire naturelle des orangers* (1818–1822, plate 52). At first sight it looks like a gourd, but on closer inspection it can be seen to be a sour orange with another distorted fruit growing out of the rind. Tanaka (1927) believed that it was a periclinal chimera, with an inner core of *Citrus medica* and an outer one of *C. aurantium*. 'Bizzaria' was thought to be extinct, but has recently been found in the citrus collection at the Villa Medici in Castello, Florence.

'Bouquetier'

Bouquet oranges, known in France as *bouquet de fleur* (flower bouquet), are especially bred for the production of the aromatic oil of neroli, an essential oil used in perfumery. The trees are smaller than most sour oranges and several cultivars have double flowers. Most trees are grown in the area around Grasse (Provence), the centre of the French perfume industry, and in Algeria and Tunisia. The most important cultivars are 'Bouquetier à Grandes Fleurs', 'Bouquetier de Nice à Fleurs Doubles', and 'Bouquetier de Grasse'. Bouquet oranges have highly fragrant flowers and round fruit with a deep orange skin. The trees grow to a height of between 2.5 and 3 metres (8–10 ft.).

'Fasciata'

'Fasciata', also called bigaradier bicolor, is an attractive form of sour orange with slightly variegated leaves and distinctive striped fruit. Young fruit are pale yellow with dark green stripes, turning to yellow with orange stripes. 'Fasciata' is presumably a chimera between two species. The Latin word *fasciata* means banded.

Bergamot (Citrus bergamia)

Bergamot trees have been cultivated in southern Europe since the seventeenth century, and the best plants are now considered to originate from Calabria in southern Italy. Some authors have treated bergamot as a cultivar of sour orange, but Gogorcena and Ortiz (1989) have shown that it is quite distinct and is probably a hybrid. (See photo on page 38.) Oil of bergamot is a key ingredient of eau de cologne and provides the distinctive flavour for Earl Grey tea.

The trees are usually grafted onto a sour orange rootstock and flower in the late spring. The young fruit are dull green, turning deep yellow as they ripen, and have very sour flesh, with many seeds. In my own experience they are less vigorous than most other citrus when containerised, but are worth growing for the wonderful scent that is released when the fruit are scratched. Bergamot trees can grow to a height of between 2.5 and 3 metres (8–10 ft.).

▲ Bouquet oranges are mainly grown for the production of neroli oil.

There are three important cultivars of bergamot. 'Femminello' (not to be confused with the lemon *Citrus limonia* 'Femminello') has fairly small round fruit with high levels of essential oil. 'Castagnaro' is very vigorous, but produces less oil than the two other cultivars. The recently introduced 'Fantastico' is claimed to be very vigorous and produces plenty of oil.

Tangelo

Tangelos (*tang-* and *-elos*) are hybrids between tangerines (strictly speaking, mandarins) and pummelos (or grapefruit).

'Minneola'
Fruit of 'Minneola' (synonym 'Honeybell') are easily recognised. They are larger than a typical mandarin, roughly spherical, but often have a very conspicuous neck and are deep reddish orange. 'Minneola' was bred in 1931 by crossing 'Dancy' tangerine with 'Duncan' grapefruit. Mature trees are quite substantial and vigorous, and have very large leaves. They produce seedless fruit when planted in isolation from other citrus trees or have very few, small seeds. The trees need plenty of heat to produce sweet fruit, but tolerate relatively low temperatures during the winter. The fruit can be harvested from February to April.

New Zealand Grapefruit

New Zealand grapefruit are also thought to be tangelos—crosses between mandarin and pummelo. They have a much lower heat requirement than true grapefruit and are well suited to the climate of New Zealand's North Island, where they are grown as an important commercial crop. They also have potential for being grown in other cooler climates and make a much better choice than true grapefruit. New Zealand grapefruit need far less heat than true grapefruit and will produce edible fruit in a greenhouse or conservatory. They grow best on trifoliate orange (*Poncirus trifoliata*) rootstock.

'Cutler Red'
'Cutler Red' was a new selection of New Zealand grapefruit in 1970. The round fruit have a deep orange skin and deep yellow-orange flesh. They are seedless if trees are kept in isolation from other citrus varieties. The

plant is readily available in New Zealand, where the fruit are harvested from October to December.

Poorman Orange (New Zealand Goldfruit)

Poorman orange, also called Poorman grapefruit, is an interesting group of citrus that appear at first sight to be grapefruit. The original plant was collected from Shanghai in 1820 by a Captain Simpson and taken to Australia, where it was named. In 1855 Sir George Grey, the island's governor, introduced the plant into New Zealand. Just over a hundred years later, in 1963, approximately 115 hectares (284 acres) of land were devoted to growing Poorman orange in New Zealand and it accounted for approximately 20 percent of the island's total citrus crop (McLintock 1966). In 1920 this group of citrus were renamed New Zealand grapefruit to reflect the great improvements that had been made in the crop. In 1981 the name was changed again to New Zealand goldfruit to improve the product's image and boost foreign exports.

'Golden Special'

For several years I grew a specimen of 'Golden Special', assuming that it was a grapefruit. There was no information to tell me otherwise and it certainly seemed to grow well in my conservatory. 'Golden Special' is actually a New Zealand grapefruit and an improved selection of poorman orange. It arose as a bud mutation of 'Morrison's Seedless' and is now one of the most widely grown citrus fruit in New Zealand. Scions are usually grafted onto trifoliate orange rootstock and bear medium-sized fruit, with a dark yellow skin and sweet, orange-yellow flesh. This plant is a good choice for anyone who wants to grow large citrus fruit in a cooler climate, because it has a much lower heat requirement than a true grapefruit and will produce large, edible fruit. It is used as a dessert fruit and for making marmalade. The fruit are harvested from August to January in New Zealand. For further information, see www.hortresearch.co.nz/files/productsandservices/citrusgermplasm/golden.pdf.

Australian Dessert Lime
(Eremocitrus glauca)

Australian dessert lime is a close relation of the genus *Citrus* and native to Queensland and New South Wales. It forms an attractive, medium-sized, thorny tree with leathery, greyish-green foliage. Seedlings can be used as a rootstock for citrus trees. The plant is remarkably drought tolerant and can last for many months without any water. It hybridises with other members of the genus *Citrus* to produce eremolemons (with lemons or 'Meyer' lemon), eremoranges (with sweet oranges), and eremoradias (with sour oranges).

◀ *Eremocitrus glauca* is an extremely attractive, weeping tree that is closely related to the genus *Citrus*. It is well adapted to a desert environment and shows good tolerance to cold and salinity.

▲ *Eremocitrus glauca* foliage.

Eremolemons

Eremolemons are bigeneric hybrids between the xerophytic Australian desert lime (*Eremocitrus glauca*) and 'Meyer' lemon. Swingle (1943) reported a case where all of the citrus plants had been removed from the U.S. Date and Citrus Station in Indio, California, with the exception of a single specimen of 'Meyer' lemon. This had freely hybridised with an Australian desert lime and produced numerous hybrid plants with yellowish, globose fruit, which he called 'Coachella' eremolemon. Swingle, quite logically, assumed that the hybrid was a cross between the *Eremocitrus* species and 'Meyer' lemon. However, it now appears that the *Eremocitrus* could also have been hybridising with the grapefruit that were growing in the vicinity, because the hybrids still appeared even after the 'Meyer' lemon tree had been removed. 'Coachella' has high tolerance to boron and saline soils.

A comparison of *Citrus* rootstocks

Rootstock	Positive Characteristics	Negative Characteristics
'Carrizo' citrange	Relatively cold hardy and high yielding. Resistant to xyloporosis.	Vulnerable to exocortis. Sensitive to salt and lime.
Citrus aurantium (sour orange)	Cold hardy. Exceptionally resistant to mal secco disease. Tolerant of phytophthora, exocortis, and xyloporosis. Produces very good quality fruit.	Very sensitive to citrus tristeza virus.
Citrus jambhiri (rough lemon)	Drought tolerant.	Vulnerable to phytophthora.
Citrus limonia (Rangpur lime)	Salt tolerant.	Vulnerable to phytophthora. Poor fruit quality.
Citrus macrophylla	Good salt and lime tolerance. Popular rootstock for lemon.	Sensitive to cold. Vulnerable to tristeza, phytophthora, and xyloporosis. With the exception of lemon, produces poor quality fruit.
Citrus reshni ('Cleopatra' mandarin)	Cold hardy. Tolerates salt and calcareous soils. Good fruit quality.	Very sensitive to phytophthora.
Citrus volkameriana (Volkamer lemon)	Tolerates mal secco disease and tristeza. Some cold tolerance.	Vulnerable to nematodes and phytophthora. With the exception of lemon, produces poor quality fruit.
Poncirus trifoliata (trifoliate orange) and its cultivar 'Flying Dragon'	Semi-dwarfing rootstock with very good cold tolerance. Resistant to tristeza, xyloporosis, and phytophthora. Produces good quality fruit.	Intolerant of salt and lime. Vulnerable to blight and burrowing nematode.
'Troyer' citrange	Relatively cold hardy. Resistant to xyloporosis.	Vulnerable to exocortis and burrowing nematodes. Sensitive to salt and lime.

9 Citrus Rootstocks

For most of their history citrus trees were grown from seed, which made it easy to establish orchards in recently colonised parts of the world such as the United States and Australia. However, the discovery of root rot disease (*Phytophthora*) in the middle of the eighteenth century led to the grafting of citrus trees onto disease-resistant rootstocks. Sour orange (*Citrus aurantium*) was used at first because it could be grown from seed and imparted good cold tolerance to the scion. The discovery of citrus tristeza disease has led to the adoption of trifoliate orange (*Poncirus trifoliata*) and several other rootstocks, such as citranges 'Troyer' and 'Carrizo'.

The rootstock has a major impact upon the growth of the scion and the quality of its fruit. Several rootstocks are available and the best choice will depend upon where you live. For example, rough lemon (*Citrus jambhiri*) thrives in hot countries and has considerable vigour but may introduce problems that outweigh these advantages, while trifoliate orange (*Poncirus trifoliata*) has good cold tolerance but may not be the right choice in a warmer climate. *Poncirus trifoliata* 'Flying Dragon' has become very popular as a rootstock for containerised citrus trees. It is very cold tolerant and has a dwarfing effect upon the grafted scion, reducing its size by approximately 50 percent. Most countries have carried out tests and have determined which are the most promising rootstocks for their climate. The accompanying table summarises the main pros and cons of the various rootstocks.

The rootstock is often very vigorous and may produce suckers. These should be removed as soon as possible, to prevent them from becoming dominant. The suckers may grow from any point below the graft union and can usually be recognised by the different leaf shape.

Sour Orange (*Citrus aurantium*)

Sour orange was the most important rootstock in worldwide use until the advent of citrus tristeza disease, to which it is very vulnerable. Sour orange tolerates phytophthora and will grow on calcareous and slightly saline soil. Many of the older orange trees in the Mediterranean basin were grafted onto this rootstock because it produces very good quality fruit. It is now illegal to use it as a rootstock in Spain for all citrus trees other than lemons. Lemon trees are hypersensitive to the tristeza virus and the cells in the area of the infection die, preventing the virus from becoming established in the rest of the plant.

Rough Lemon (*Citrus jambhiri*)

Citrus jambhiri is native to the foothills of the Himalaya in India, but was widely distributed by Portuguese and Spanish explorers. It became naturalised in several citrus-growing regions, including South Africa, Florida, and the Caribbean. Rough lemon forms a very vigorous plant with an extensive root system and, grown by itself, makes a large, spreading tree with numerous thorns. The fruit are orange-yellow, roughly spherical with a very uneven surface. They are unlikely to be mistaken for anything else.

This species is widely used as a rootstock for lemon trees and produces very vigorous trees with plenty of fruit; however, on the down side, the fruit it produces have a thicker skin and yield less juice than fruit grown on trees grafted onto other rootstocks. Rough lemon is susceptible to several diseases and can be damaged by frosts, but is so vigorous that it will usually recover during the following year. It is salt tolerant and tolerates tristeza, but the grafted scions may suffer from granulation. Grafted trees tend to grow very vigorously when they are young, but start to decline after approximately fifteen years. The trees continue to deteriorate and often succumb to disease

'Milam' is widely used as a rootstock for lemon trees.

when they are twenty or more years old. The cultivar 'Milam' has good resistance to the burrowing nematode.

Rangpur Lime (Citrus limonia)

Rangpur lime is unrelated to the true limes and is probably a hybrid between a mandarin and another species. It tolerates drought, salt, and calcareous soils, but is vulnerable to cold weather. Although it is resistant to tristeza disease, it is vulnerable to nematodes and exocortis.

Citrus macrophylla

Citrus macrophylla (synonym 'Macrophylla') is often used as a rootstock for lemon trees in California and Spain, but is unsuitable for use in colder climates. It produces a very vigorous tree and tolerates alkaline and saline soil conditions. On the down side, it is sensitive to cold, and grafted trees have a tendency to lean over.

'Cleopatra' Mandarin (Citrus reshni)

Also known as spice tangerine, *Citrus reshni* originated in India and reached Florida in the middle of the nineteenth century. It is an attractive, thornless tree with dark green leaves and small reddish-orange fruit. These are too small to have any commercial value, but the tree makes a very ornamental plant and the seedlings can be used as a rootstock. The fruit are approximately 2.5 centimetres (1 in.) across and will last for up to a year if left on the tree. The plant has good salt tolerance and will grow on shallow, calcareous soils. It is very sensitive to phytophthora and is vulnerable to nematodes and water logging. Tanaka assigned 'Cleopatra' mandarin to *Citrus reshni*.

Trifoliate Orange (Poncirus trifoliata)

Trifoliate orange is widely used as a rootstock because of its resistance to cold and heat. A native of central and northern China, this spiny, deciduous shrub has trifoliate leaves and bears flowers on the previous year's wood (members of the genus *Citrus* flower on the current year's wood). The plant can be grown as a hardy ornamental shrub and is used in Brazil as an extremely effective burglarproof hedge. Trifoliate orange has been crossed with the sweet orange to produce citranges.

The Chinese and Japanese appear to have used trifoliate orange as a rootstock for several centuries, but the famous plant hunter Robert Fortune first recorded its use for this purpose in 1848. The graft is extremely successful and the trifoliate rootstock grows faster with a citrus scion than an intact trifoliate seedling of the same age. *Poncirus trifoliata* is widely used as a rootstock in colder countries, but produces smaller fruit than other rootstocks and has a dwarfing effect on the scion.

◀ *Poncirus trifoliata* (trifoliate orange) forms a small deciduous tree. It is widely used as a rootstock and tolerates cold and wet soil conditions.

▶ *Poncirus trifoliata* produces small yellow fruit with extremely bitter flesh and many seeds.

Poncirus trifoliata 'Flying Dragon'

Poncirus trifoliata 'Flying Dragon' is a scary plant when it is young and is not exactly child friendly. Young plants have long, wavy branches covered with small trifoliate leaves and scythe-shaped thorns. When mature, 'Flying Dragon' forms a small deciduous tree, up to 3 metres (10 ft.) high with a dense spreading crown of spiny branches. The plant has found favour as a dwarfing rootstock for citrus plants, but needs to be treated with considerable care when grown as a specimen plant. The fruit are small and roughly spherical, and have a wrinkled golden-yellow skin.

'Flying Dragon' originated in Japan and is mainly used as a rootstock for containerised plants. It is a dwarf form of *Poncirus trifoliata* and reduces grafted citrus trees to between 20 and 33 percent of their normal size. It is, like the normal trifoliate orange, cold tolerant and will grow in moderately wet soil.

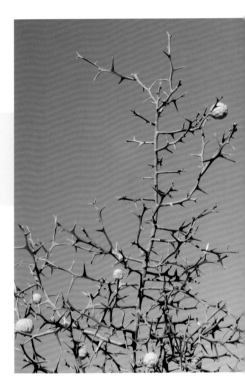

▶ *Poncirus trifoliata* 'Flying Dragon' has wavy stems and sickle-shaped thorns. It too is used as a rootstock.

Volkamer Lemon (*Citrus volkameriana*)

Volkamer lemon is highly resistant to mal secco disease and widely used as a lemon rootstock in Italy, where it has been known since the seventeenth century. It was named after Johann Volkamer, author of the famous *Nürbergische Hesperides* (1708–1714). *Citrus volkameriana* is probably a hybrid between a lemon and a sour orange. It forms a small tree, with slightly toothed, elliptical leaves and has a few thorns when it is young. The lemon-shaped fruit have a reddish-orange rind and yellow-orange flesh, with a few seeds and a slightly bitter, but pleasant taste. Volkamer lemon is highly sensitive to phytophthora and should not be used as a rootstock where the disease is present. Fruit quality tends to be rather poor, with considerable granulation, but the species does impart tolerance of tristeza, exocortis, and xyloporosis. It is used as rootstock for 'Eureka' lemons in Australia.

Citranges

Citranges are hybrids between trifoliate orange (*Poncirus trifoliata*) and sweet orange (*Citrus sinensis*) and will tolerate much lower temperatures

than other edible citrus plants. They have an upright habit and, when mature, large young shoots arch out from the top, forming a crown-shaped tree. The foliage is usually trifoliate and much larger than that of a trifoliate orange, although some cultivars have single leaves like sweet orange. The fruit are mainly held at the bottom of the tree and have a rather petrol-like smell when they are scratched. They are too acidic to be eaten directly, but produce a pleasant juice and can be used for cooking. Citranges have been widely adopted as rootstocks in the United States, but perform badly on calcareous and saline soils. The trees have rather lethal spines, but can be grown in areas that are too cold for true citrus plants.

Citrange cultivars range from the semi-deciduous 'Etonia' to the almost entirely evergreen 'Troyer'.

'Carrizo' produces better yields than its sibling 'Troyer' and is consequently growing in popularity. It forms a rounded tree with strong erect shoots and bears large quantities of small, round, orange fruit measuring approximately 6 centimetres (2¼ in.) across. It is sensitive to salt.

'Etonia' forms a very large, upright tree with very spiny, arching branches. The plant is semi-deciduous and has large trifoliate leaves. The light orange fruit are produced from October to December.

'Troyer' has become a very popular rootstock and the majority of Spanish plants are now grafted onto it. Grown as a specimen tree, 'Troyer' produces large quantities of small light orange fruit, measuring approximately 5 × 6.5 centimetres (2 × ½ in.). The fruit are very acid and somewhat bitter, but have a very attractive fragrance. Like 'Carrizo', 'Troyer' is unsuitable for areas with saline or alkaline soils.

▲ Citranges form large spiny bushes, with strong, arching branches. The upper branches have less foliage than the lower.

▶ The lower branches of a citrange bush have more foliage than the upper.

Questions and Answers

Q: I've just taken my orange tree indoors for the winter and all of the leaves have fallen off. What should I do?

A: Citrus trees do not like sudden changes of temperature or humidity and often respond by dropping all of their leaves. Centrally heated houses or conservatories have a very dry atmosphere, which is unsuitable for growing citrus trees. The plant will produce new foliage, but it is important to reduce the temperature in the room where you are keeping it and maintain a high humidity with a water atomiser.

Q: My citrus tree is looking very unhealthy and the leaves are turning yellow. What have I done wrong?

A: It sounds as though you might have been overwatering it. If this is the case, let the soil dry out and then give the plant plenty of water in one go. Resist the temptation to water it again until you are certain that it is needed. Whatever you do, resist the temptation to give your plant a bit of water every day.

Q: It's been quite cold recently and the leaves of my 'Washington' navel orange have turned a bronzy brown colour.

A: It sounds as though the tree has been damaged by frost. It should recover, but in the future make sure you keep it somewhere warmer. Citrus trees need a minimum temperature of 10°C (50°F) to grow successfully, although they will tolerate lower temperatures for a short time.

Q: The leaves of my lemon tree are covered with oval brown shells. The leaves are very sticky and are covered with large patches of black mould.

A: This sounds like scale insects. Remove the mature insects with cotton wool soaked with methylated spirits. Then spray the plant with Provado Ultimate Bug Killer in the United Kingdom or Admire in the United States. You will need to spray at least twice a year to keep the insects at bay.

Q: I live in California and the fruit on my 'Eureka' lemon are turning white on the upper side. What is causing this?

A: It sounds like sunburn. There is little that you can do other than to erect some shade over the tree during the hottest months of the summer.

Q: There are lot of green shoots at the bottom of my potted citrus tree. They have three leaflets and look completely different from those of the citrus tree. What are they?

A: These are probably suckers from the rootstock of your tree. If they have three leaflets they are probably from a trifoliate orange rootstock. Cut them off at ground level and rub out any that appear on the side of the stem.

Q: The leaves on my citrus tree are turning yellow, but still have green veins. What is the cause?

A: The yellowing is probably the result of chlorosis, and there are two possible causes. The first is that there is too much lime in your tap water and this is building up in the soil. The safest way of curing this is to gradually add flowers of sulphur to the compost until the soil pH has been reduced. The sulphur converts the calcium to sulphate (gypsum) and allows the plant to take up essential nutrients from soil. The other cause could be a mineral deficiency. If the former solution doesn't work, try watering the plant with a special balanced citrus fertiliser.

Q: My 'Washington' navel orange has produced a very long, flattened shoot, which is over 1 metre (3 ft.) long. Why has it done this?

A: The growth is probably a water shoot. It is quite natural and it won't do any damage, but it will make the tree look rather unbalanced. Prune the shoot to approximately one-third of its current length, so that it is in proportion to the others. It will eventually become round like the other branches.

Q: I am unhappy about the shape of my lime tree. All of the branches are at the bottom of the tree and it looks ugly. What can I do?

A: There is a limit to what you can do with any type of tree. I always advise people to buy a standard with a long vertical stem rather than one than is branched at the bottom. You might be able to improve the shape of your tree with a bit of careful pruning. Select a strong upright stem and remove all of the other stems with a pair of secateurs. Then prune the remaining stem so that a bud is facing outwards. The bud should start growing and form a strong vertical stem. It will never be perfect, but should have a more attractive shape as it continues to grow.

Q: The top part of my citrus tree has died, but there are green suckers growing from the pot. What can I do about this?

A: It sounds as though the scion, the grafted upper part of your tree, has died and the rootstock has started to grow its own shoots. If this is the case, you have two choices. You can let the rootstock grow and use it to produce seeds for rootstocks, or you can try grafting a scion from another of your trees onto it. This is quite a skilled job, but you have nothing to lose.

Q: My orange tree had plenty of flowers in the spring, but most of the fruit have fallen off. Why has this happened?

A: This completely natural process is nothing to worry about. Citrus trees always produce far more fruit than they could possibly support. It is nature's way of thinning out the crop. It can also happen if you forget to water the plant.

Q: I've had an orange tree for several years, but it has not produced any fruit. What am I doing wrong?

A: Unfortunately, there is no simple answer to this question. The most likely reason is that it needs feeding. Citrus trees need to be fed regularly if they are to grow well. Water your plant with a balanced citrus fertiliser every couple of weeks and see if it produces fruit. I notice that you live in northern France. It may be too cold there for your orange tree. You may have better results if you can overwinter the tree in a warm greenhouse or a conservatory.

Where to See Citrus

Citrus trees are common in many Mediterranean gardens and it would be impractical to list all of them here, but there are a number of world-class gardens that should be visited if possible. At the top of the list comes the royal Palace of Versailles, closely followed by the Villa Medici di Castello in Italy.

Austria

Schloss Schönbrunn-Haupteingang
Schönbrunner, Schloss-Strasse
A-1130 Vienna
Tel: +43 (1) 811 13 239
Web site: www.schoenbrunn.at

Schönbrunn Palace has the second largest baroque orangery in the world. The building was started in 1754 and is 189 metres (620 ft.) long and 10 metres (33 ft.) wide. A collection of citrus trees is placed out in the palace gardens during the summer, but the orangery is now used for receptions and as a dining room.

France

Château de Versailles
Versailles
Tel: +33 (1) 30 83 78 00
Web site: www.chateauversailles.fr/en/

The Palace of Versailles has one of the most famous gardens in the world and an iconic collection of citrus trees. There are over a thousand orange trees, planted in the famous green wooden Versailles containers. Grown as standards with a spherical top, the trees are taken outside in May and returned to the protection of the orangery in October. The gardens are extremely busy during the summer and are best visited early in the morning.

Château de Saint-Loup
79600 Saint-Loup Lamairé
Tel: +33 (5) 49 64 81 73

Web site: www.chateaudesaint-loup.com

The beautiful Château de Saint-Loup is home to a collection of approximately a hundred citrus trees, composed of twenty-seven different cultivars. The trees are grown outdoors in the eighteenth-century orangery court and taken indoors for the winter.

Palais Carnolès

3, Avenue de la Madone
Menton
Tel: +33 (4) 93 35 49 71
Web site: www.menton.com/gardens/carnoles.htm

Formerly the summer residence of the princes of Monaco, the seventeenth-century palace of Carnolès now houses the town's museum of modern art. It has a beautiful renaissance-style garden and one of the largest collections of citrus trees in Europe. There are approximately four hundred citrus trees from eighty different taxa. The garden is closed on Tuesdays and during bank holidays.

Italy

Boboli Gardens
(Giardino di Boboli)

Piazza Pitti
1, Florence
Tel: +39 (055) 294 883
Web site: www.firenzemusei.it/boboli

Niccolò Pericoli designed this spectacular renaissance garden for Eleonora of Toledo, wife of Duke Cosimo de Medici, in 1549. The garden has a large collection of citrus trees, which are overwintered in the limonaia (citrus greenhouse) and spend their summer on the isoletto, an island in the middle of the lake.

Secret Gardens
(Giardini Segreti)

Villa Borghese
Piazza Scipione Borghese 5
00197 Rome
Tel: +39 (06) 82 077 304
Web site: www.villaborghese.it

These private gardens were created in the seventeenth century for Cardinal Scipione Borghese. Visitors must book in advance.

Villa Hanbury

Corso Montecarlo 43
18038 La Mortola Inferiore
Ventimiglia
Tel: +39 (184) 229 507
Web site: www.amicihanbury.com

The famous Villa Hanbury has a number of mature citrus trees in the garden.

Villa Medici di Castello

Castello, Via di Castello 47
50141 Florence
Tel: +39 (055) 454 791
Web site: www.polomuseale.firenze.it/musei/villacastello

The Medici citrus collection is one of the largest in the world and includes many rare cultivars, such as 'Bizzaria' citron. The Villa was built for Cosimo dé Medici, the Grand Duke of Tuscany, and designed by Niccolò Pericoli some time prior to 1550 A.D. The collection includes approximately five hundred specimens of potted citrus tree, including several that were illustrated in Risso and Poiteau's famous book *Histoire naturelle des orangers* (1818–1822). The Oscar Tintori citrus nursery is a short distance away.

Netherlands

Paleis Het Loo Nationaal Museum

Koninklijk Park 1
7315 JA Apeldoorn
Tel: +31 (55) 577 24 00
Web site: www.paleishetloo.nl

Sometimes referred to as the Dutch Versailles, Het Loo Palace was originally the summer residence of the House of Orange. Construction of the house started in 1684, shortly before its owner, William of Orange, became King William III of England. The palace is home to the Dutch National Citrus Collection, which mainly consists of specimens and cultivars of sour orange (*Citrus aurantium*). Approximately thirty of the trees are two hundred or more years old.

Spain

Royal Alcázar Palace

Patio de Banderas s/n
C.P. 41004
Seville
Tel: +34 (954) 50 23 24
Web site: www.sevillaonline.es/english/seville-city-centre/alcazar-palace.htm

The beautiful Alcázar Palace is a World Heritage site and one of the best examples of Moorish architecture in the world.

Turkey

Tuzcu Citrus Collection

c/o The Faculty of Agriculture
Çukurova University
01330 Adana

This large collection includes 866 accessions of Citrus and related genera. It was established in 1972.

United Kingdom

There are very few citrus collections on display in the British Isles, but plenty of orangeries to visit. Sadly very few of them are used to house citrus trees and the great majority have been turned into restaurants. It is strange that at this time of comparative wealth there are no large collections of citrus trees in the British Isles, other in a few commercial nurseries.

Birmingham Botanical Gardens and Glasshouses
Westbourne Road
Edgbaston
Birmingham B15 3TR
England
Tel: +44 (121) 454 1860
Web site: www.
birminghambotanicalgardens.org.uk

Approximately one dozen mature citrus trees are planted in the borders of the Victorian glasshouse.

Carew Manor
Church Road
Beddington, Sutton
London
Tel: +44 (20) 8770 4781
Web site: www.sutton.gov.uk/leisure/heritage/Beddington/carewmanor.htm

Nothing remains of the orangery now, save for the north wall, but oranges were being grown here during the middle of the sixteenth century. Sir Francis Carew is recorded as having purchased lemon trees when he was in Paris between 1561 and 1562. The orange trees died during the winter of 1739–40 and the southern wall was demolished in 1820, but it is worth going just to see the medieval hammer-beam roof in the Grade I listed hall. Carew Manor is now a school, but there are guided tours during the spring and summer.

Ham House
Ham Street, Ham
Richmond-upon-Thames
Surrey TW10 7RS
England
Tel: +44 (20) 8940 1950
Web site: www.nationaltrust.org.uk

The orangery at Ham House was first built in 1677, but is now greatly altered.

Hampton Court Palace
East Molesley
Surrey KT8 9AU
England
Tel: +44 (844) 482 7777
Web site: www.hrp.org.uk/HamptonCourtPalace

While hardly comparable with the collection of citrus at Versailles, the trees at Hampton Court are still worth seeing. The trees are planted in white barrels, with steel handles for lifting.

Hanbury Hall (National Trust)
School Road, Hanbury
Droitwich Spa
Worcestershire WR9 7EA
England
Tel: +44 (1527) 821 214
Web site: www.nationaltrust.org.uk

This is one of the few places in the British Isles where it is possible to see a functioning orangery. The trees are still very young, but they are kept in the building during the winter and taken outside during May.

Kensington Palace State Apartments

Kensington Gardens
London W8 4PX
England
Tel: +44 (844) 482 7777
Web site: www.hrp.org.
uk/KensingtonPalace

The beautiful Kensington Palace orangery was built in 1704 for Queen Anne and designed by Sir Christopher Wren. It was one of the first purpose-built orangeries in the British Isles and home to the citrus collection from Kew Palace. The citrus trees were displayed on the large Portland Stone platform at the front of the orangery. The platform also made it easier to wheel the citrus trees in and out of the building. The orangery is currently used as a tearoom.

Margam Country Park

Margam
Port Talbot SA13 2TJ
Wales
Tel: +44 (1639) 881 635
www.npt.gov.uk/margampark

The massive orangery at Margam Country Park measures 83 metres (275 ft.) long and is the longest such building in Britain. It was designed by Anthony Keck and built between 1787 and 1793. The estate maintained a collection of citrus trees until the beginning of the Second World War, when the orangery was requisitioned for use by the American army. The trees were left outside and died during the following winter. A new collection was established after the war.

Mount Edgcumbe House and Country Park

Cremyll, Torpoint
Cornwall PL10 1HZ
England
Tel: +44 (1752) 822 236
Web site: www.mountedgcumbe.gov.
uk

The elegant country house at Mount Edgcumbe overlooks Plymouth harbour and has had a long association with citrus trees. The first citrus trees were collected in Turkey by Richard, the second Baron Edgcumbe (1716–1761), in 1744. Three years later his brother George, later the First Earl Edgcumbe (1721–1795), was Captain of HMS Salisbury, a fifty-gun warship in the Royal Navy. The ship's surgeon, James Lind, is famous for proving that citrus fruit could be used to prevent scurvy, a debilitating disease that affected many sailors of the time (Sutton 2003).

The orangery was built in 1760 and once housed the best collection of citrus trees in Britain. It suffered serious damage during the Second World War and the trees in the original collection were killed. The trees were replaced in 1990 and are grown outside in the Italian Garden. The house and garden were sold to Plymouth City Council and Cornwall County Council in 1971 and are open to the public. The orangery is currently used as a restaurant, but forms a beautiful backdrop to the small citrus collection.

Peckover House and Garden

North Brink
Wisbech
Cambridgeshire PE13 1JR
England
Tel: +44 (1945) 583 463
Web site: www.nationaltrust.org.uk

A Georgian townhouse with an attractive orangery and several large citrus trees.

Powis Castle

Welshpool
Powys SY21 8RF
Wales
Tel: +44 (1938) 551 929
Web site: www.nationaltrust.org.uk

Powis Castle is famous for its Italianate gardens and has a late eighteenth-century orangery.

Royal Botanic Gardens, Kew

Richmond
London TW9 3AB
England
Tel: +44 (20) 8332 5000
Web site: www.kew.org

The famous orangery at Kew was originally built for Augusta, the Dowager Princess of Wales, in 1761. In 1841 the palace gardens became the Royal Botanic Gardens and the citrus collection was moved to Kensington Palace. The iconic orangery has been restored on several occasions, but is now used as a restaurant. A small collection of citrus trees can still be found growing in the Temperate House at Kew.

Saltram House

Plympton
Plymouth
Devon PL7 1UH
England
Tel: +44 (1752) 333 500
Web site: www.nationaltrust.org.uk

The orangery is home to a large collection of citrus. It includes twenty large trees and one that is almost 9 metres (30 ft.) tall.

Victoria and Albert Museum

Cromwell Road
London SW7 2RL
England
Tel: +44 (20) 7942 2000
Web site: www.vam.ac.uk

This has to be one of the most exciting examples of how citrus trees can be used for architectural effect in a modern garden. The John Madejski Garden was opened to the public in July 2005 and dominates the centre courtyard. Twenty-two mature lemon trees have been arranged around an Italianate courtyard with an elliptical pool in the centre. The trees are planted in translucent metre-wide glass containers, which are illuminated with blue light at night. The lemon trees are replaced with clipped holly during the cold winter months. Entrance is free.

United States

Anna Scripps Whitcomb Conservatory

Belle Isle Botanical Society
8109 East Jefferson
Detroit, Michigan 48214
Tel: +1 (313) 331 7760
Web site: www.bibsociety.org

Originally built in 1904, this large dome-shaped glasshouse is 26 metres (85 ft.) high. It is home to one of the largest collections of orchids in the United States. In the Second World War a large number of rare orchids were rescued from the British Isles to prevent them from being lost during the blitz. These were stored in the glasshouse. The South wing houses a collection of tropical economic plants, including orange trees, coffee, and bananas.

California Citrus State Historic Park

1879 Jackson Street
Riverside, California 92504
Tel: +1 (909) 780 6222
Web site: www.parks.ca.gov

This interesting park was opened in 1993 and houses a large collection of commercial citrus trees. At the centre is a recreation of a Californian citrus growing community, complete with a packing shed, offices, and a grower's home. The park has approximately seventy-five varieties of citrus on display. The California Citrus Non-Profit Management Corporation manages the 75 hectares (185 ac) of citrus groves.

Citrus Variety Collection

Department of Botany and Plant Sciences
University of California Riverside
Riverside, California 92521
Web site: www.citrusvariety.ucr.edu/

The University of California, Riverside, has one of the largest collections of citrus in the world, with approximately nine hundred accessions from the genus Citrus and twenty-seven related species. The collection belongs to the university and is, strictly speaking, not open to the public. If you would like to visit please, contact the curator at +1 (951) 827 4619.

Longwood Gardens

P. O. Box 501
Kennett Square, Pennsylvania 19348
Tel: +1 (610) 388 1000
Web site: www.longwoodgardens.org

Longwood Gardens is one of the world's great gardens. It has an amazing 1.8 hectares (4.5 ac) of greenhouses, including the orangery, which was originally built to overwinter citrus trees.

Missouri Botanical Garden

4344 Shaw Boulevard
St. Louis, Missouri 63110
Tel: +1 (314) 577 9400
Web site: www.mobot.org

The impressive Linnean House, a brick-built orangery, was constructed in 1882 to house tender plants and to overwinter citrus trees and palms. It is the oldest continuously operated glasshouse in the United States and currently home to a large collection of camellias.

The Parent Washington Navel Orange Tree

On the corner of Arlington and Magnolia Avenues
Riverside, California

This remarkably healthy specimen is the sole survivor of the original three 'Washington' navel orange trees that were sent to Riverside in 1873 by the United States Department of Agriculture in Washington. Two of the trees survived, with one being moved to the Glenwood Hotel (now the Mission Inn) and the other to its existing site at the junction of Arlington and Magnolia Avenues. All 'Washington' navels in the United States are descended from this pair of trees. The Glenwood tree died some time ago, but the other is alive and kicking at the grand old age of 134 years old.

Suppliers

The following list is not comprehensive, but it should provide a good starting point for finding citrus trees, planters, fertiliser, and other products. Readers should contact the companies listed before they pay a visit. Most wholesale nurseries will not deal with the general public. If you want to buy a small number of citrus trees, you should contact a retail nursery.

Citrus Trees

Australia

Bob & Geoff Poulters' Citrus Trees Nursery
Elder Street
Heatherton, Victoria 3202
Tel: +61 (3) 9551 2597

Fitzroy Nurseries
P.O. Box 859
Rockhampton, Queensland 4700
Tel: +61 (7) 49272 3888
(retail)

Golden Grove Queensland
Bruce Highway
Torbanlea, Queensland 4662
Tel: +61 (7) 4129 4147
(wholesale and retail)

Loxton Vine & Citrus Nursery
886 Kingsbury Road
Loxton, South Australia 5333
Tel: +61 (8) 8584 5544
Web site: www.pippos.com
(wholesale and retail)

Swane's Nurseries
490 Galston Road
Dural, New South Wales 2158
Tel: +61 (2) 9651 1322
Web site: www.swanes.com
(retail)
Also at: 237 Marsden Road
Carlingford
Tel: +61 (2) 9871 1699
Also at: 80 Port Hacking Road
Sylvania
Tel: +61 (2) 9522 7086

Turner's Garden Centre
473 Miles Platting Road
Rochedale, Brisbane 4123
Tel: +61 (7) 3341 5214

Web site: www.turnersgardencentre.com.au
(retail)

The company motto is 'We'll sell you a lemon'.

France

Agrumes du Soleil (SCEA)
San Giusto
20215 Vescovato
Tel: +33 (4) 95 36 70 04

Pépinières Bachès
Mas Bachès
66500 Eus
Pyrénées-Orientales
Tel: +33 (4) 68 96 42 91
E-mail: bachesbene@aol.com

Pépinière Hodnik
1 place du 19 Mars 1962
45700 St-Maurice-sur-Fessard
Tel: +33 (2) 38 97 84 59
Web site: www.hodnik.com

Pépinière Michel Dufau
62 rue Harguett
40320 Eugénie les Bains
Tel: +33 (5) 58 51 18 54
Web site: www.agrumes-dufau.com

Pépinières Viala Rémy
Lieu-dit Paterno
20290 Borgo
Tel: +33 (4) 95 36 07 65
Web site: www.pepinieres-viala.com

Serres Horticoles Vergnaud
Route d'Aslonne Danlot
86370 Vivonne
Tel: +33 (5) 49 43 43 70
Web site: www.serres-horticoles-vergnaud.com

Germany

Citrus Gärtnerei
Bernhard Voss
Moorende 149
21635 Jork
Tel +49 4162/356 or 942524
Web site: members.aol.com/agrumivos2/citrue.htm

Flora Toskana
Schillertr. 25
89278 Nersingen OT Strass
Tel: +49 (07308) 92 833-87
Web site: www.flora-toskana.de

Italy

Italy is one of the largest citrus growing countries in the European Union and many of its trees are exported to other parts of Europe.

Azienda Agricola Pannitteri & C.
C. da Porticelli - S.P. 135
95032 Belpasso (CT)
Tel: +39 (095) 791 3562
Web site: www.pannitteri.com
Web site: www.aranciarosaria.it

This nursery is famous for its blood oranges.

Cuciti Vivai Trinacria Vitis
Via Palmara, 1/7
98057 Milazzo (ME)
Tel: +39 (090) 929 5036
Web site: www.cucititrinacriavitis.it

Fratelli Ingegnoli
Viale Pasubio 13/23 (Porta Volta)
20154 Milan
Tel: +39 (022) 901 5121
Web site: www.ingegnoli.it

Sicilia Verde
Via del Mare Contrada Acquitta
98050 Terme Vigliatore (ME)
Tel: +39 (090) 974 0944
Web site: www.siciliaverde.it/index.
htm

Vivai Mangiapane
Contrada Cerasia, 29
88029 Lamezia Terme (CZ)
Tel: +39 (968) 209 543
Web site: www.mangiapanevivai.it

Vivai Oscar Tintori
Via Tiro a Segno 55
51012 Castellare di Pescia (PT)
Tel: +39 (0572) 429 191
Web site: www.oscartintori.it

Vivaio Luciano Noaro
Via Vittorio Emanuele 151
18033 Camporosso (IM)
Tel: +39 (184) 288 225
Web site: www.noarovivaio.it

New Zealand

Copperfield Nursery
221 Snodgrass Road
Te Puna, RD2 Tauranga
Tel: +64 (7) 552 5780
Web site: www.copperfield.co.nz
(wholesale)

Kwan Citrus Nursery
410 Kerikeri Road
Kerikeri 0470
Tel: +64 (9) 407 8628

Switzerland

Eisenhut Vivai
CH-6575 San Nazzaro
Tel: +41 (91) 795 18 67
Web site: www.eisenhut.ch
(retail)

United Kingdom

While interest in citrus is growing
in the United Kingdom, there are no
wholesale nurseries and the majority
of plants are either grafted by the
nursery owners or imported from
other parts of the European Union.

The Citrus Centre
West Mare Lane
Pulborough
West Sussex RH20 2EA
Tel: +44 (1798) 872 786
Web site: www.citruscentre.co.uk
(retail)

Cross Common Nursery

The Lizard
Helston
Cornwall TR12 7PD
Tel: +44 (1326) 290 668
Web site: www.crosscommonnursery.co.uk
(retail)

David's Exotic Plants UK

Tel: +44 (1227) 711 897
Web site: www.davids-exoticplants.co.uk
(mail order only)

Global Orange Groves UK

Horton Road
Horton Heath
Wimborne
Dorset BH21 7JN
Tel: +44 (1202) 826 244
Web site: www.globalorangegroves.co.uk
(retail) Supply certified virus-free plants.

Reads Nursery

Hales Hall
Loddon
Norfolk NR14 6QW
Tel: +44 (1508) 548 395
Web site: www.readsnursery.co.uk
(retail)

United States

There are extremely strict controls on the transport of citrus within the United States. Plants must be purchased locally if you live in an area where citrus are grown commercially. At the time of writing, legislation had been introduced to control citrus canker in Florida. The entire state was under quarantine and plants could not be shipped outside the state.

Acorn Springs Farms

2488 Hickey Road
Hallsville, Texas 75650
Tel: +1 (888) 442 2676
Web site: www.acornsprings.com
(retail and wholesale—do not ship to Arizona, California, or Florida)

Brite Leaf Citrus Nursery

480 CR 416 South
Lake Panasoffkee, Florida 33538
Fax: +1 (352) 793 3674
Web site: www.briteleaf.com
(wholesale, Internet, and mail order)

Flying Dragon Citrus Nursery

3973 Loretto Road
Jacksonville, Florida 32223
Tel: +1 (904) 880 5026
Web site: www.flyingdragoncitrusnursery.com
(retail)

Four Winds Growers
P.O. Box 3538
Fremont, California 94539
Web site: www.fourwindsgrowers.
com
(wholesale, Internet, and via
California retail nurseries)

Greenfield Citrus Nursery
2558 East Lehi Road
Mesa, Arizona 85213
Tel: +1 (480) 830 8000
Web site: www.greenfieldcitrus.com)
(retail—only ship within Arizona)

Harris Citrus
10721 Highway 39 South
Lithia, Florida 33747
Tel: +1 (813) 655 3370
Web site: www.harriscitrus.com
(retail)

Louie's Nursery
16310 Porter Avenue
Riverside, California 92504
Tel: +1 (951) 780 7841
Web site: www.louiesnursery.com
(retail)

Parkview Nursery
3841 Jackson
Riverside, California 92503
Tel:. +1 (951) 351 6900
(retail)

Pell's Citrus and Nursery
400 Doyle Road
Osteen, Florida 32764
Tel: +1 (800) 459 8897
Web site: www.pellcitrus.com
(retail)

Thompson Nursery
2823 Pleasantview Drive
Weslaco, Texas 78596
Tel: +1 (888) 667 2644
Web site: www.thompsoncitrus.com
(retail and wholesale—do not ship to
Arizona, California, or Florida)

Ty Ty Nursery
4723 US Highway 82 West
P.O. Box 130
Ty Ty, Georgia. 31795
Tel: +1 (800) 972 2101
Web site: www.tytyga.com
(retail—do not ship to Arizona,
California, Florida, or Texas)

Planters and Versailles Containers

Hardwood planters are quite
expensive, but they will last
considerably longer than those
made from softwood. It is always
wise to ask about the origin of the
hardwood and only buy containers
made from timber that was
sourced from a correctly managed,
sustainable plantation. Many
furniture importers are cautious
about revealing the source of their
wood, due to the negative publicity
that it can attract.

United Kingdom

Ailsa Wood Products

Penwhapple Bridge
Old Dailly, Girvan
Ayrshire KA26 9TH
Scotland
Tel: +44 (1465) 871 287
Web site: www.ailsadirect.co.uk
(hardwood Versailles planters from
Keruin wood)

Barlow Tyrie

Braintree
Essex CM7 2RN
Tel: +44 (1376) 557 600
Web site: www.teak.com
(natural teak Versailles planters)

The Chelsea Gardener

125 Sydney Street
London SW3 6NR
Tel: +44 (207) 352 5656
Web site: www.chelseagardener.com
(white painted Versailles planters)

Sylvan Enterprises

The Mills, Pleasley Vale
Mansfield
Nottinghamshire NG19 8RL
Tel: +44 (1623) 812 565
Web site: www.sylvan-furniture.
co.uk
(high-quality Versailles planters
from European oak or western red
cedar)

The Topiary Shop

Brett's Garden Centre
Chelmsford Road
White Roding near Great Dumow
Essex CM6 1RF
Tel: +44 (845) 230 6008
Web site: www.topiaryshop.co.uk
(galvanised, stainless steel, and
FSC-certified oak planters. Also sell
a limited range of citrus trees.)

United States

Authentic Provence

522 Clematis Street
West Palm Beach, Florida 33401
Tel: +1 (561) 805 9995
(wide range of attractive planters
made from metal and wood)

Barlow Tyrie

1263 Glen Avenue, Suite 230
Moorestown, New Jersey 08057
Tel: +1 (856) 273 7878
E-mail: USsales@teak.com
(high-quality Versailles containers
from teak)

Brattle Works

Cambridge, Massachusetts 02138
Tel: +1 (617) 864-2110
Web site: www.brattleworks.com
(Versailles containers of western red
cedar with plain or trelliswork sides)

Citrus Fertiliser

United Kingdom

Chempak Products
Hillgrove Business Park
Nazeing
Essex EN9 2BB

Supplies two different fertilisers. Their winter fertiliser has a ratio of 18–18–18 with magnesium oxide and trace elements, while the summer formulation is 24–14–14.

Global Orange Groves UK
Horton Road
Horton Heath
Wimborne
Dorset BH21 7JN
Tel: +44 (1202) 826 244
Web site: www.globalorangegroves.co.uk

This nursery offers two fertilisers. The winter formulation is 20–20–20 and the summer is 25–15–15. Both fertilisers have seven trace elements added.

Reads Nursery
Hales Hall
Loddon
Norfolk NR14 6QW
Tel: +44 (1508) 548 395
Web site: www.readsnursery.co.uk

The nursery sells a 21–7–21 fertiliser with added trace elements (manganese, boron, zinc, copper and molybdenum) and chelated iron.

United States

Lutz Super Citrus Tablets
Lutz Corporation
501 Ford Street
Oregon, Illinois 61061
Tel: +1 (800) 203 7740
Web site: www.lutzcorp.com/citrustrees

The manufacturer claims that these tablets will provide sufficient fertiliser for 12 months.

Miracle-Gro Fruit & Citrus Tree Fertilizer Spikes
Miracle-Gro Shake 'n Feed
Continuous Release Citrus, Avocado, & Mango Plant Food
Tel: +1 (888) 295 6902
Web site: www.miraclegro.com

Vigoro Citrus and Avocado Granular Plant Feed
Web site: www.vigoro. com

This fertiliser is available in 3.5-, 20-, and 40-lb. bags from Home Depot and Viva!

Biological Control

Agralan
The Old Brickyard
Ashton Keynes
Swindon
Wiltshire SN6 6QR
England
Tel: +44 (1285) 860 015
Web site: www.agralan.co.uk
(carnation tortrix moth traps)

Becker Underwood
P.O. Box 667
801 Dayton Avenue
Ames, Iowa 50010
United States
Tel: +1 (515) 232 5907
Web site: www.beckerunderwood.
com

The company supplies a range of
nematode-based products such as
Nemasys H and BioVector. These are
particularly effective in controlling
in soil-inhabiting pests such as vine
weevils.

Becker Underwood France
Z.I. En Jacca
10, Chemin de la Plaine
31770 Colomiers, Toulouse, France
Tel: +33 (534) 508 650

Becker Underwood UK,
Harwood Industrial Estate
Harwood Road
Littlehampton
West Sussex BN17 7AU
England
Tel:+44 (1903) 732 323.

Terracotta Pots

There are many manufacturers
of terracotta pots. These vary
considerably in quality, but it is very
much a case of 'you get what you
pay for'. Frost-resistant pots are not
essential, but hand-made pots are
less likely to crack and tend to look
more attractive.

Whichford Pottery
Whichford, Nr. Shipston-on-Stour
Warwickshire, CV36 5PG
England
Tel: +44 (1608) 684 416
Web site: www.whichfordpottery.
com.

Glossary

beladi The name for common orange in North Africa.

bud mutation A spontaneous change in the genetic make up of a bud. The affected bud can be grafted onto a rootstock and produce a new cultivar with better characteristics than its parent. Most citrus cultivars have arisen as bud mutations. Radiation is sometimes used to stimulate mutation in the bud meristem.

calyx The sepals of a flower. The number of sepals in citrus plants can range from three to five, but is usually five.

carnauba An edible, naturally occurring wax derived from the carnauba wax palm (*Copernica prunifera*). Carnauba (E-903) is one of the hardest waxes known.

chimera The combination of tissues from two different genetic sources in the same organism.

citrange A hybrid between sweet orange (*Citrus sinensis*) and tri-foliate orange (*Poncirus trifoliata*).

citrangequat A hybrid between (*C. sinensis* × *Poncirus trifoliata*) and *Fortunella japonica* or *F. margarita*.

citrangor A hybrid between *Citrus sinensis* and (*C. sinensis* × *Poncirus trifoliata*).

comuna The name for common orange in Spain.

comune The name for common orange in Italy.

corolla The petals of a flower. Citrus plants may have between five and eight petals, but usually five.

cortex The outer part of a stem or root.

crenulate Having an edge with small rounded teeth.

criolla The name for common orange in Argentina and Uruguay.

dripline The maximum extent of the foliage of a plant, where rain falls on the ground.

ellipsoid A solid object with an oval profile.

eremolemon A hybrid between Australian dessert lime (*Eremocitrus glauca*) and 'Meyer' lemon.

eremorange A hybrid between Australian dessert lime (*Eremocitrus glauca*) and sweet orange.

globose Shaped like a ball.

granulation A condition where the juice vesicles harden and lose their flavour. It often occurs in plants that have been grafted onto a rough lemon (*Citrus jambhiri*) rootstock.

limb sport A mutation of a branch or shoot that is genetically different from the rest of the tree.

limequat The cross between the Mexican lime (*Citrus aurantifolia*) and a kumquat (*Fortunella margarita* or *F. japonica*).

limonene A colourless terpene that gives citrus fruit their distinctive smell. Limonene is a very effective solvent and can be used as paint stripper and an insecticide.

limonin A white crystalline material that occurs in citrus fruit.

minneola A cross between 'Duncan' grapefruit and 'Dancy' mandarin. The fruit look like large mandarin oranges, but are less sweet and may not appeal to children.

mutation A spontaneous change to the genetic material, which usually occurs during cell division. Plant breeders often use radiation to increase the incidence of mutation, but it can be a double-edged sword, producing bad as well as good characteristics.

navel orange A form of sweet orange with a small secondary fruit developed at the end of the main one. Navel oranges grow best in countries with a Mediterranean climate.

neck The end of the fruit where it is attached to the tree.

nipple A protuberance at the end of a fruit. Lemons often have a prominent nipple at the stylar end of the fruit.

nucellar Derived from an embryo which is genetically identical to one parent and thus a clone (vs. an embryo that is the result of sexual reproduction).

oblate Said of fruit having a larger circumference at the equator than from pole to pole.

oil glands A common feature in most parts of the citrus flower and the surface of their fruit. Pure 'waterless' citrus oil is an extremely powerful solvent and capable of removing grease, melting plastic, and even removing glue! A detergent has to be added to the oil to enable it to be mixed with water.

orangelo A hybrid between a citrange and a grapefruit (*C. paradisi*).

orangequat A hybrid between a sweet orange and a kumquat.

orangery A purpose-built structure for growing oranges and other citrus plants.

petiole The stalk of a leaf. In some species the petiole is a broad, leaf-like structure and often as large as the true leaf.

phytophthora A serious, water-borne disease that can kill citrus plants. Good drainage is essential because there is no cure and most citrus plants are now grafted onto a resistant rootstock.

scion The aerial part of a grafted plant. The scion bears the foliage and the fruit.

segments The subdivisions of a citrus fruit. Derived from the carpels, these contain juice-filled sacs or vesicles.

shellac A naturally occurring thermoplastic polymer, which is produced by the lac insect (*Coccus lacca*). It is used to prevent post-harvest decay of fruit.

stamens The male part of the flower, which includes the anthers and supporting filaments. The stamens are usually fused into groups of three or more and vary in number from approximately 20 to 40.

stigma The receptive part of the pistil, which collects pollen for fertilisation.

style The part of the pistil that supports the stigma. Pollen grains produce a tube that grows through the style to reach the ovule.

stylar end The part of the fruit furthest from the stalk.

tangelo A hybrid between grapefruit (*Citrus paradisi*) and mandarin (*C. reticulata*).

tangerine Originally a marketing term coined for 'Dancy' mandarin as the fruit were originally sourced from Tangiers.

tangor A hybrid between sweet orange (*Citrus sinensis*) and mandarin (*C. reticulata*).

trifoliate orange A very popular rootstock, which imparts a high cold tolerance to the tree. It is widely used as a rootstock in Japan but has vicious thorns.

USDA The United States Department of Agriculture.

water shoot A very vigorous shoot that is occasionally produced by a citrus tree and which affects the symmetry of the bush. Water shoots are often flattened and may grow 50 cm or more in a single season.

wax A shiny carnauba- or shellac-based coating applied to commercially produced citrus fruit before they are exported.

Bibliography

Literally hundreds of scientific papers have been published about citrus, as you would expect for one of the world's most important crops.

Joseph Risso and Pierre Poiteau's *Histoire naturelle des orangers* (1818–1822) is probably the most important source of information for the old citrus cultivars. The book is beautifully illustrated with stipple engravings, but includes many cultivars that hardly differ from one another. For example, there are four forms of bergamot, namely, *Bergamottier Ordinare*, *Bergamottier a Fruit Toruleux*, *Bergamot a Petit Fruit*, and *Bergamotte Mellarose*. There are unusual forms of lemon: pear-shaped (*Lemonier Imperiale*), spindle-shaped (*Limonier a Fruit Fusiforme*), oblong-shaped (*Limonier a Fruit Oblong*), and fluted-rind (*Limonier a Fruit Canaiculé*). The majority of the illustrated plants are sour oranges, sweet oranges, lemons, and limes; grapefruit had not been introduced when the book was written and mandarins had only just been introduced from China. The shaddock makes an appearance (*Pompelmouse Chadec*), as do the pummelo (*Pompoleon Ordinaire*) and several citrons (*Cédratrier a Gros Fruit*). There are also two blood oranges: *Oranger à Feuilles Etroites* and *Oranger à Fruit Tardif*. Risso and Poiteau's book was revised on several occasions during the early nineteenth century and an original first edition commands a high price. A modern facsimile has been published by the French company Connaissance et Mémoires (www.connaissance-memoires.com) for a more reasonable €400.

J. W. Webber and L. D. Batchelor's four-volume series *The Citrus Industry* was last published in 1976 (with W. Reuter), but is still considered to be the definitive work on citrus. It is heavy going but encyclopedic in its coverage of the citrus industry and the different species. The text is also available on the Internet at www.lib.ucr/agnic/webber.

Many readers will find *Citrus of the World* (Cottin 2002) of considerable value. It lists hundreds of synonyms for different cultivars and gives the generally accepted name. It extends to 58 pages and can be downloaded as a free PDF document.

Finally, James Saunt's *Citrus Varieties of the World* (2000) is invaluable for his encyclopedic coverage of commercial citrus varieties.

Andrews, H. C. 1824. *The Botanist's Repository*. 9: 608.

Araújo, E. F. de, L. P. de Queiroz, and M. A. Machado. 2003. What is *Citrus*? Taxonomic implications from a study of cp-DNA evolution in the tribe Citreae (Rutaceae subfamily Aurantioideae). *Organisms Diversity and Evolution* 3 (1): 55–62.

Aromatic Plant Project. 2004. What Makes an Essential Oil Smell the Way It Does? www.aromaticplantproject.com/articles_archive/citrus_essential_oils.html

Becerra-Rodríguez, S., V. M. Medina-Urrutia, M. M. Robles-González, and T. Williams. 2007. Performance of various grapefruit (*Citrus paradisi* Macf.) and pummelo (*C. maxima* Merr.) cultivars under the dry tropic conditions of Mexico. *Euphytica*.

Bowen, H. V. 2006. *The Business of Empire. The East India Company and Imperial Britain, 1756–1833*. Cambridge University Press.

Bowl, P. 2004. *Gardens of the Roman World*. London: Frances Lincoln.

Brown, C. G. 2003. *Mount Edgcumbe* (Visitor Guide).

Cottin, R. 2002. *Citrus of the World: A Citrus Directory*. Version 2.0.

France: National Institute of Agricultural Research (INRA) and the Centre of International Co-operation and Research on Agricultural Development (CIRAD). www.corse.inra.fr/sra/citrus.htm#English

Davidson, R., and W. Lyon. 1979. *Insect Pests of Farm, Garden, and Orchard*. John Wiley and Sons.

Edwards, S. 1817. *The Botanical Register* 3: plate 211.

Evelyn, J. 1658. *The Diary of John Evelyn*. Vol. 2 (1647–1676).

Ferrari, G. 1646. *Hesperides: sive, de malorum aureorum cultura et usu libri quatuor*. Rome: Hermanni Scheus.

Florida Department of Citrus. May 2007. Citrus Reference Book. www.floridajuice.com/pdfs/RB2007.pdf.

Food and Agriculture Organization (FAO). 2007. *Citrus Fruit: Fresh and Processed. Annual Statistics 2006*. www.fao.org/es/esc/en/15/238/highlight_243.html.

Gallesio, G. 1811. *Traité du Citrus*. Paris: Louis Fantin.

Gogorcena, Y., and J. M. Ortiz. 1989. Characterisation of sour orange (*Citrus aurantium*) cultivars. *Journal of the Science of Food and Agriculture* 48 (3): 275–284.

Hodgson, R. W. 1967. Horticultural varieties of citrus. In *The Citrus Industry*, eds. W. Reuther, H. J. Webber, and L. D. Batchelor. 1: 431–591

Hooker, W. J. 1834. Observations on some of the classical plants of Sicily. *The Journal of Botany* 1: 98.

Horticulture and Food Research Institute. 2005. 'Golden Special'. New Zealand National Citrus Germplasm Collection. www.hortresearch.co.nz/ files/productsandservices/ citrusgermplasm/golden.pdf

Hume, H. H. 1957. *Citrus Fruits*. New York: MacMillan.

International Association for Horticultural Science 2004. *International Code for the Nomenclature of Cultivated Plants*. 7th ed. Belgium: International Association for Horticultural Science.

Laräs, A. 2005. *Gardens of Italy*. London: Frances Lincoln.

Lind, J. 1953. *A Treatise of the Scurvy. In Three Parts. Containing an Enquiry into the Nature, Causes, and Cure of that Disease.* Edinburgh.

Lushington, A. W. 1910. The genus *Citrus*. *Indian Forester* 36: 323–353.

Lysons, D. 1792. *The Environs of London*. Volume 1: *County of Surrey*.

Mabberley, D. J. 1997. A classification for edible *Citrus* (Rutaceae). *Telopea* 7 (2): 167–172.

Mabberley, D. J. 1998. Australian Citreae with notes on other Aurantioideae (Rutaceae). *Telopea* 7(4): 333–344.

McLintock, A. H. 1966. *An Encyclopaedia of New Zealand.* Wellington: R. E. Owen.

Morton, J. F. 1987. *Fruits of Warm Climates*. Miami: J. Morton.

Nati, P. 1674. *Florentina phytologica observatio de malo limonia citrata-aurantia Florentiae vulgo la bizzarria.*

Needham, J. 1986. *Science and Civilisation in China.* Volume 6, *Biology and Biological Technology*. Part 1. *Botany*. Cambridge University Press.

Nelson, H. 1814. *The Letters of Lord Nelson to Lady Hamilton; With a Supplement of Interesting Letters by Distinguished Characters.* London: Thomas Lovewell and Company. London. 1: 257.

Nicolosi, E., Z. N. Deng, A. Gentile, S. La Malfa, G. Continella, and E. Tribulato. 2000. Citrus phylogeny and genetic origin of important species as investigated by molecular markers. *Biomedical and Life Sciences* 100 (8): 1155–1166.

Oliver, P. 1993. *Success with Citrus*. Poole, England: Global Orange Groves.

Pang, X. M., C. G. Hu, and X. X. Deng. 2007. Phylogenetic relationships within *Citrus* and its related genera as inferred from AFLP markers. *Genetic Resources and Crop Evolution* 54 (2): 429–436.

Pliny the Elder. 77 A.D. *Naturalis Historia*. Eds. John Bostock and H. T. Riley. London: Taylor and Francis, 1855.

Rieger, M., G. Krewer, P. Lewis, M. Linton, and T. McClendon. 2003. Field evaluation of cold hardy citrus in coastal Georgia. *Horttechnology* 13 (3): 540–544.

Risso, J. A., and P. A. Poiteau. 1818–1822. *Histoire naturelle des orangers*. Paris: Audot.

Ruggieri, G. 1935. La diversa resistanza alla defogliazione prodotta dal vento in alcune specie di 'Citrus' in rapporto alla struttura anatomica del picciòlo. *Bollettino dello Roma Stazione di Patologia Vegetale* 15: 169–199.

Samson, J. A. 1980. *Tropical Fruits*. London: Longman Group.

Saunt, J. 2000. *Citrus Varieties of the World*. 2d ed. Norwich, England: Sinclair International Business Resources.

Scora, R. W., and J. Kumamoto. 1983. Chemotaxonomy of the genus *Citrus*. In *Chemistry and Chemical Taxonomy of the Rutales*, eds. P. G. Waterman and M. F. Grundon. London: Academic Press. 343–351.

Sloane, Sir Hans. 1707–1726. *A Voyage to the Islands Madeira, Barbados, Nieves, S. Christophers, and Jamaica*. London.

Spiegel-Roy, P., and E. E. Goldschmidt. 1996. *The Biology of Citrus*. Cambridge University Press.

Stenzel, N. M. C, and C. S. V. J. Neves. 2004. Rootstocks for 'Tahiti' lime. *Sci. agric. (Piracicaba, Braz.)* 61 (2).

Stone, B. C., J. B. Lowry, R. W. Scora, and J. Jong. (1973. *Citrus halimii*: a new species from Malaya and peninsular Thailand. *Biotropica* 5: 102–110.

Sutton, G. 2003. Putrid gums and 'Dead Men's Cloath's': James Lind aboard the *Salisbury*. *Journal of the Royal Society of Medicine* 96 (12): 605–608.

Swingle, W. T. 1943. The botany of *Citrus* and its wild relatives of the orange subfamily (family Rutaceae, subfamily Aurantioideae). In *The Citrus Industry*, eds. H. J. Webber and L. D. Batchelor. Berkeley: University of California Press. 1: 129–474.

Tanaka, T. 1927. Bizzarria—a clear case of periclinal chimera. *Journal of Genetics* 18: 77–85.

Tanaka, T. 1928a. Revisio aurantiacearum (I). *Bulletin de la Société botanique de France* 75: 708–715.

Tanaka, T. 1928b. Revisio aurantiacearum (II). Two new genera and new combinations of Rutaceae-Aurantieae from Papua. *Arnold Arboretum Journal* 9: 137–144.

Tanaka, T. 1929. Revisio aurantiacearum (IV). *Chalcas*, a Linnean genus which includes many new types of Asiatic plants. *Soc. Trop. Agric. Jour.* 1: 23–44.

Tanaka, T. 1930. Revisio aurantiacearum (III). Compendium des espêces indo-chinoises d'aurantiacées. *Bulletin du Muséum national d'Histoire naturelle* 2: 157–164.

Theophrastus. 310 B.C. *Historia Plantarum.*

Tintori, G., and S. Tintori. 2000. *Ornamental Citrus Plants.* Edifir, Firenze.

Tolkowsky, S. 1938. *Hesperides: A History of the Culture and Use of Citrus Fruits.* London: John Bale, Sons and Curnow.

Trabut, L. 1902. Une nouvelle tangérine, La Clémentine. *Le gouvernement général de l'Algérie* (Dir. de l'Agriculture Bulletin) 35: 21–35.

Train, J. 2006. *The Orange— Golden Joy.* Easthampton and Woodbridge: Antique Collector's Club.

Valder, P. 1999. *The Garden Plants of China.* London: Weidenfield and Nicholson.

Volkamer, J. C. 1708–1714. *Nürbergische Hesperides, oder gründliche Beschreibung der edlen Citronat-Citronen und Pomerantzen-Früchte.* 2 vols. Nürnberg.

Waldheim, L. 1996. *Citrus.* Tucson, Arizona: Ironwood Press.

Webber, H. J., and L. D. Batchelor, eds. 1943. *The Citrus Industry.* Volume 1: *History, Botany, and Breeding.* 1st ed. Berkeley and Los Angeles: University of California.

Woodfield, P. 1991. Early buildings in gardens in England. Archaeology papers presented to a conference at Knutson Hall, Northamptonshire, April 1988. Council for British Archaeology Research Report No 78. 123–137.

Woods, M., and A. S. Warren. 1996. *Glass Houses: A History of Greenhouses, Orangeries and Conservatories.* Aurum Press.

Index

Bold face indicates photo pages.

A

Adam's apples (pummelos), 19
'Adam's Apple' (citron), 62, 134
Aleurocanthus woglumi, 88
Alexander the Great, 13
Algerian mandarin. See 'Commune'
(clementine)
'Algerian Tangerine'. See 'Commune'
(clementine)
Alhambra Palace, 9
'American Wonder'. See *Citrus pyriformis*
'Ponderosa'
anthocyanins, 102, 105, 120
ants, 90–91
'Aoshima', 116, **117**
aphids, 91
Arabs, 9, 15, 16, 18
'Aurantiata'. *Citrus medica* 'Aurantiata'
Australian dessert lime, 148–149
'Australique'. See 'Ortanique'
Avington Park orangery, 23

B

'Bahia'. See 'Washington' navel
bartender's lime. See West Indian lime
'Bearss', 30, 135

Beddington, 21
beladi, 98
bergamot, 38, 146–147. See also *Citrus
bergamia*
oil of, 37, 146
'Berna'. See 'Verna'
beta-carotene, 102
Bianchetti crop, 129
bigarade. See *Citrus aurantium*
bigaradier bicolor. See 'Fasciata'
'Biondo Comune', **96**, 98
Birmington Botanical Gardens, 23
'Bitrouni', **133**, 133
'Bizzaria', 16, 62, 144, 145–146
blood orange, 45, 47, 105–107, 120
bonsai, 141
bouquet de fleur, 146
'Bouquetier', 146
'Bouquetier à Grandes Fleurs', 146
'Bouquetier de Grasse', 146
'Bouquetier de Nice à Fleurs Doubles',
146
bouquet oranges, **146**
breeding, 27–29, 47
British East India Company, 16, 19
'Buddha's Hand' citron, 42, **43**. Also see
Citrus medica var. *sarcadactylis*
budwood, 28

C

Cacoecimorpha pronubana, 93
'Calamondin', 44, **141**, 141–142
California State Citrus Park, 58
'Campbell', 101
Cape lemon. See rough lemon
'Cara Cara', 101–102, **102**, 105
Carew, Sir Francis, 21, 62
'Carey's Eureka'. See 'Garey's Eureka'
carnation tortrix moth, **93**, 93–95
Carnauba wax, 12
'Carrizo', 78, 83, 86, 87, 150, 156
'Castagnaro', 147
Celebes papeda. See Citrus celebica
'Chandler', 125, 125–126
'Changsha', 63, 119
'Ch'ang-sha'. See 'Changsha'
chimera, 16, 145
China, 13, 15, 19, 35
Chinese citron. See Citrus medica
   'Aurantiata'
chinotto. See Citrus aurantium var.
   myrtifolia
'Chinotto Grande', 145
'Chinotto Piccolo', 145
'Chinotto Crispifolia', 145
'Chinotto Buxifolia', 145
Christmas tangerine. See 'Dancy'
cidro digitado. See 'Buddha's Hand'
citrange, 119, 150, 155–156
citrangequat, 119
×Citrofortunella, 142
×Citrofortunella microcarpa. See
   'Calamondin'
citron, 9, 13–15, 138–139
Citropsis, 25
Citrus, 25, 29
Citrus aurantifolia, 18, 31, 134, 136,
   142, 143
Citrus ×aurantifolia. See C. aurantifolia

Citrus aurantium, 17, 25, 31, 36, 83,
   144, 144–146, 150, 152
  var. canaliculata, 145
  var. myrtifolia, 145
  var. salicifolia, 145
Citrus ×aurantium. See C. aurantium
Citrus bergamia, 37, **38**, 146–147
citrus blackfly, 88
citrus cachexia viroid, 86
citrus canker, 82, 115
Citrus celebica, 31
Citrus clementina, 30, 111
Citrus deliciosa, 30, 107, 108–109
citrus exocortis viroid (CEVd), 85, 153
Citrus grandis, 31
citrus greening, 83
Citrus halimii, 31
Citrus hystrix, 25, 30, 31, 38, 45
Citrus ichangensis, 31, 63, 118, 137
Citrus indica, 31
Citrus jambhiri, 136, 150, 152
Citrus ×jambhiri. See C. jambhiri
Citrus latifolia, 18
Citrus latipes, 31
citrus leaf miner, 89
Citrus limon, 31
  var. lumia. See C. lumia
Citrus ×limon. See C. limon
Citrus limonia, 136, 150, 153
Citrus lumia, 133, 134
Citrus macrophylla, 150, 153
Citrus macroptera, 31
Citrus maxima, 31, 124–128, **124**
citrus mealy bug, 88
Citrus medica, **14**, 31, 32, 138–139, 145
  'Aurantiata', 139
  var. digitata. See 'Buddha's Hand'
  'Etrog', 138
  var. sarcodactylis, **138**, 138. Also see
   'Buddha's Hand'

Citrus ×*meyeri*. See 'Meyer'

Citrus micrantha, 31

Citrus nobilis, 30, 107, 109

Citrus paradisi, 31, 119

citrus peel, 46

Citrus pyriformis 'Ponderosa', **133**, 133

Citrus reshni, 30, 150, 153

Citrus reticulata, 10, 30, 31, 107, 109, 116, 141

citrus rust mite, 89

citrus scab, 84

Citrus sinensis, 31, 98–107, 144, 155

Citrus tachibana, 31

Citrus tangerina, 30

citrus tristeza virus (CTV), 84–85, 125, 132, 152, 153

Citrus unshiu, 30, 107, 115–118

Citrus volkameriana, 150, 155

citrus whitefly, 87

'Clausellina, 116–117

clementine, 10, 30, 46, 109, 111–115 Spanish, 112

'Clemenules'. See 'Nules'

'Clemenvilla'. See 'Nova'

'Cleopatra', 30, 83, 135, 150, 153

'Coachella', 149

'Cocktail Grapefruit', 113, 126

cold hardiness, 63, 116, 118

cologne, eau de, 36

Columbus, Christopher, 18

commercial uses of citrus, 36–38

'Commune' (clementine), 111, 111–112

'Commune' (orange), 99

compost, 49–51

comuna, 98

comune, 98

conservatories, 70–72

cooking with citrus, 38–45

cottony cushion scale, 88

criolla, 98

Crusades, 15, 18, 136

CTV. See citrus tristeza virus

cultivar names, 33

Curaçao, 37

'Cutler Red', 147–148

'Cutter', 101

D

'Dancy', 110, **110**, 147

'Dancy Tangerine'. See 'Dancy'

'De Nules'. See 'Nules'

degreasant, 36

'Delta', 101

Deuterophoma tracheiphila, 86

Dialeurodes citri, 87

diseases, 47

'Doble Fina', 107

dolce, 105

douce, 105

drainage, 65

drying disease, 86

dry rot, 62

'Duncan', **20**, **121**, 147

E

Earl Grey tea, 38, 146

'Ellendale', **11**, 112, **112**

Eremocitrus glauca, 148–149, **149**

eremolemon, 149

eremoradias, 149

'Etonia', 156

'Etrog'. See *Citrus medica* 'Etrog'

Eucitrus (subgenus), 30, 31, 32

'Eureka'. See 'Garey's Eureka'

European carnation moth, **93**, 93–95

'Eustis', 63, 142–143, **143**

Evelyn, John, 21
'Excelsior', 101
exocortis. See citrus exocortis disease
    (CEVd)

F

'Fasciata', 16, 144, 146
Feast of Tabernacles, 138
feeding, 53
'Femminello' (bergamot), 147
'Femminello' (lemon), 129
'Femminello Commune'. See
    'Femminello' (lemon)
'Femminello Ovale'. See 'Femminello'
    (lemon)
Ferrari, Giovanni, 62
fertiliser, 53–56, 71
'Fina'. See 'Commune' (clementine)
fingered citron. See 'Buddha's Hand'
'Flame', 120
floral structure, 26–27
'Flying Dragon'. See *Poncirus trifoliata*
    'Flying Dragon'
Forest Stewardship Council (FSC), 73
'Fortune', 108, 113
Fortune, Robert, 139, 154
Fortunella, 119, 139–142
Fortunella crassifolia, 139, 140
Fortunella hindsii, 139
Fortunella japonica, 139, 142
Fortunella margarita, 139–140, 143
'Foster', 122
'Four Seasons'. See 'Calamondin'
fragrance, 12, 14, 26, 138
'Frost' (valencia), 101
frost damage, 63, 74, 129
'Frost Lisbon', 28, 130, 131
'Frua', 113, 126

fruit, 26, 45, 79–80
fruit drop, 27
fungus, 82, 84, 86, 87, 88
fungicide, 12

G

Gallesio, George, 134
'Garey's Eureka', 45, 129–130, 155
'Goldfruit'. See 'Oroblanco'
'Golden Special', 24, 45, 148
Grand Marnier, 19
grafting, 78–79
granulation, 152, 155
grapefruit, 19–20, 38, 119–123. See also
    Citrus paradisi
  New Zealand, 45, 147–148
  pink, 130
  red, 130
grapefruit salad, 43
Grasse (France), 146
greenhouse, 10, 60, 66, 69–70
greenhouse red spider mite, 92
greening disease, 83
Grey, Sir George, 148
Gwynne, Nell, 19

H

Hampton Court Palace, 23
Hanbury Hall, 23
'Hart's Late'. See 'Valencia'
'Hart's Tardiff'. See 'Valencia'
'Honeybell'. See 'Minneola'
honey tangerine. See 'Murcott'
Hooker, William, 105
'Hudson', 28, 122, 123
Hume, Sir Abraham, 16, 17, 108
hybrid names, 31–32

I

Icerya purchasi, **88**
Ichang papeda. See also *Citrus
    ichangensis*
'Improved Meyer', 45, 61, 132
Indian wild orange. See *Citrus indica*
insect pests, 87–91

J

'Jaffa'. See 'Shamouti'
'Jaffa Red Pomelo'. See 'Chandler'
'Jaffa Sunrise'. See 'Star Ruby'
'Jaffa Sweetie'. See 'Oroblanco'
Japan, 18, 115
juice, 20, 35, 37, 39, 46, 100, 107, 121

K

kaffir lime. See *Citrus hystrix*
'Kao Pan', 124
'Kai Yai', 124
Kensington Palace, 23
Key lime. See West Indian lime
Key lime pie, 39, 40
Khasi papeda. See *Citrus latipes*
kid glove tangerine. See 'Dancy'
'King of Siam'. See 'King'
'King', 109
king mandarin, 30
'Kinokawa', 124, **124**
'Kinokawa Buntan'. See 'Kinokawa'
kumquat, 44, 45, 119, 139–142. Also see
    Fortunella

L

La Bizzaria. See 'Bizzaria'
Lady Grey tea, 38
'Lakeland', 143
'Lane Late', **27**, 102

'Laraha', 37
leaf drop, 67
leaf structure, 25
lemon, 9, 15, **34**, 45, 129–134. See also
    Citrus limon
lemonade, 44
Le Nôtre, Andre, 22
lime (fruit), 9, 18, 45, 134–137. See also
    Citrus aurantifolia
lime (mineral), 56
limequat, 142–143
limeys, 42
limoncello, 44
Limoni crop, 129
limonin, 37, 47, 102
'Lisbon', 28, 45, **130**, 130–131
Louvre, Palace of the, 21
lycopene, 102, 120

M

'Macrophylla'. See *Citrus macrophylla*
Majorca, 8, 16, **34**, **75**, 144
makrud, 38
'Makrut', 137. See also Thai lime
mal secco, 86, 150, 155
Malta orange, **105**, 106
'Maltaise de Tunisie'. See 'Maltaise
    Sanguine'
'Maltaise Sanguine', 106
mandarin, 10, 16–18, **17**, 30, 35, 45,
    107–119. See also *Citrus deliciosa*,
    C. nobilis, *C. reticulata*, *C. unshiu*
    Cambodian. See mandarin, king
    common, 107, 109
    Indochinese. See mandarin, king
    king, 107, 109
    Mediterranean, 107,108–109
    Satsuma. See Satsuma

yellow king. See mandarin, king

'Mandora'. See 'Ortanique'

Margam orangery, 23

Maria, Queen Henrietta, 21

marmalade, 40, 41–42

'Marsh', **20**, 47, **120**, 121–122, **122**

'Marsh Seedless'. See 'Marsh'

'Marumi', 140, 142

Median-apple, 13

'Meiwa', 63, **140**, 140–141

Melanesian papeda. See *Citrus macroptera*

'Melogold', 126

Mexican lime. See West Indian lime

'Meyer', 32, 61, 63, **131**, 131–132, 149

Meyer, Frank, 131

mice, 91

'Milam', **87**, **152**, 153

'Minneola', 107, 147

'Miyagawa', 117

miyagawa wase, 117

'Moro', **47**, **106**, 106

'Morrison's Seedless', 148

Mount Edgcumbe, 22

Mozoe lemon. See rough lemon

'Mr Johns Longevity', 119

'Murcott', **11**

myrtle-leaved orange, 145. Also see
  Citrus aurantium var. *myrtifolia*

N

'Nagami', 45, 63, **139**, 139–140, **140**

naranja, 98

naranja amarga. See *Citrus aurantium*

'Navelina', 102–103

nematodes, 49, 86–87, 92, 153

neroli, oil of, 36, 146

New Zealand goldfruit. See Poorman
  orange

New Zealand grapefruit, 147–148

'Newhall', 103

Nôtre, André Le, 22

'Nova', 108, 113–114, **114**

'Nules', 45, 108, **114**

nucellar seedlings, 28

nutrients, 53–56

O

oil (citrus), 27, 36, 38, 39

'Olinda' (valencia), 101

orange, 9

  beladi, 98

  blood, 45, 47, 105–107, 120

  bouquet, 145

  common, 98–101

  comune, 98

  criolla, 98

  navel, 46, 101–104

  pigmented. See orange, blood

  sugar, 105

  trifoliate. See *Poncirus trifoliata*

orange citron. See *Citrus medica*
  'Aurantiata'

orangequat, 63, 139

orangeries, 13, 16, 20–23

'Oroblanco', 124, 126, 127

'Ortanique', **27**, 115

Otiorhynchus sulcatus, 91

oval kumquat, 139

overwatering, 64–66

overwintering, 66–69

'Owari', **2**, 45, **46**, 63, **64**, 117–118, **118**

P

Padua, 21

'Page'. See 'Tahiti'

Panonychus citri, 89

Papeda (subgenus), 30, 31, 32

'Pear Lemon', 134

pectin, 38, 40, 44

Penicillium mould, 81–82

perfume, 36, 109, 146

'Pero del Commendatore'. See 'Pear Lemon'

'Persian'. See 'Tahiti'

Persian apple, 13

petitgrain, oil of, 36, 109

photosynthesis, 25, 55

Phyllocnistus citrella, **89**

Phyllocoptruta oleivora, 89

Phytophthora, 66, 74, 76, 82–83, 151

'Pink Marsh'. See 'Thompson'

pink navel. See 'Cara Cara'

pips, 77

plant labels, 60

plant selection, 59-61

Pliny the Elder, 14

'Poir du Commandeur'. See 'Pear Lemon'

Poiteau, Pierre 17, 62

'Pomelit', 124

pomelo. See grapefruit

'Pomme d'Adam'. See 'Adam's Apple'

'Pomme du Paradis'. See 'Adam's Apple'

Pompeii, 15

pompelmous. See pummelo

Poncirus trifoliata, 25, 83, 119, 150, 153–154, **154**

  'Flying Dragon', 150, 153, 154–155, **155**

'Ponderosa', **133**, 133

Poorman grapefruit. See Poorman orange

Poorman orange, 148

'Portugaise'. See 'Maltaise Sanguine'

Portugal oranges, 19

pots, 48, 50, 51–53, 65, 66

Primofiori crop, 129

pruning, 75, 76–77

pummelo, 19, **120**, 124–128. See also *Citrus maxima*

Q

queen of oranges, 106

R

Radopholus citrophilus, **87**

Raleigh, Sir Walter, 21

'Rangpur', 135, 136, 150

razzlequat, 64

'Redblush'. See 'Ruby'

red citrus mite, 89

'Reed', **28**

'Rio Red', 122

Risso, Joseph, 17, 62

'Rivers' Late'. See 'Valencia'

Rivers, Thomas, 101

'Riverside Navel'. See 'Washington'

Rodier, Clement, 111

Rose's lime juice cordial, 42

root rot, 65. Also see *Phytophthora*

rootstocks, 60, **77**, 151–156

rough lemon, 136, 150, 151, 152–153

round kumquat. See 'Meiwa'

Royal Botanic Gardens, Kew, 23

royal mandarin. See 'Temple'

'Ruby', 122–123

'Ruby Red'. See 'Ruby'

S

salt, 57, 150, 152, 153, 156

'Salustiana', 98

'Sanguinelli'. See 'Spanish Sanguinelli'

'Sanguinelli Negro'. See 'Spanish Sanguinelli'

'Sanguinello', 106–107

'Sanguinello Commune'. See 'Sanguinello'

Satsuma, 30, 107, 115–118

scale insects, 89–90, **90**

scion, 60, 78–79, 83

scurvy, 42

seed propagation, 47

Seville orange, 16, **27**, 40, 45

shaddock. See pummelo

Shaddock, Captain Phillip, 19

'Shamouti', **27**, **99**, 99

shellac, 12

Siamese pink pummelo, 125

Siamese sweet pummelo, 125, 126

'Sinton', 119

slow decline, 86

small-flowered papeda. See *Citrus micrantha*

'Smith's Early Navel'. See 'Navelina'

snails, 92

soft drinks, 36

soil, 49, 57, 74

acid, 57, 74

calcareous, 54, 136, 152, 153, 156

sooty mould, 82, 87, 91

sour orange, 9, 16, 45, 144–149, 152.
See also *Citrus aurantium*

'Spanish Sanguinelli', 107

spice tangerine. See 'Cleopatra'

spreading decline, 87

St Clements Church, 19

St Clements drink, 19

'Star Ruby', 20, 28, 101, **120**, **123**, 123

subtropical climate, 73–75

suckers, 76–77, 151

'Sucreña', 105

'Sunrise'. See 'Star Ruby'

'Sweetie'. See 'Oroblanco'

sweet orange, 9, 13, 18–19, 45, 98–107.
See also *Citrus sinensis*

Swingle, Walter, 30–31, 32, 142

T

Tachibana orange. See *Citrus tachibana*

'Tahiti', **18**, 30, **43**, 45, 135, **135**

'Tambor'. See 'Ortanique'

Tanaka, Tyôzaburô, 30, 32

tangelo, 127, **147**

tangerine, 10, 30, 109–110

tangor, 109, 112, 115

'Tarocco', **27**, 45, 107, **107**

'Tarocco del Francofonte', 107

'Tarocco del Muso', 107

'Tarocco Rosso', 107

'Tavares', **143**

taxonomy, 29–33

'Telfair', 119

temperate climate, 10, 61–69

temple mandarin, 30

'Temple', 118–119, **119**

Tetranychus urticae, 92

Thai cuisine, 38, 45

Thai lime. See *Citrus hystrix*

Theophrastus, 13

'Thomasville', 119

'Thomson', **104**

'Thomson Improved'. See 'Thomson'

'Thompson' (grapefruit), 29, **120**, 123

'Thong Dee', 124

Tibbetts, Eliza, 103

'Topaz'. See 'Ortanique'

'Troyer', 78, 86, 150, 156

U

Ugli®, 127, 127–128, 128
University of California, Riverside, 33, 113, 125, 126
unshiu mikan, 115

V

'Valencia', **27**, 29, 37, 45, 100–101
'Valencia Late'. See 'Valencia'
'Variegated Eureka', 132
Verdelli crop, 129
Verdi crop, 132
'Verna', 132
Versailles, Palace of, 22
Versailles containers, 22, 72–73
'Villafranca', 133
vine weevils, 91–92
viruses, 74, 81–86
vitamin C, 42, 107, 119
Volkamer lemon, 83, 86, 150
Volkamer, Johann, 155

W

'Washington', 26, 30, 45, 47, 103–104, **104**
'Washington Early'. See 'Navelina'
'Washington Navel'. See 'Washington'
water shoots, 76–77
watering, 64–66
West Indian lime, 136. See also *Citrus aurantifolia*
'Wheeny', **128**, 128–129
'White Marsh'. See 'Marsh'
'Whitney'. See 'Marsh'
willow-leaved orange, 145
winter, 54, 63, 66
Wren, Sir Christopher, 23

X

xyloporosis, 86, 150

Y

yellow dragon disease, 83
Yichang orange. See *Citrus ichangensis*

Z

zipper-skin tangerine. See 'Dancy'